TEACHER'S PET PUBLICATIONS

LITPLAN TEACHER PACK
for
Bridge to Terabithia
based on the book by
Katherine Paterson

Written by
Janine H. Sherman

© 1997 Teacher's Pet Publications
All Rights Reserved

This **LitPlan** for Katherine Paterson's
Bridge to Terabithia
has been brought to you by Teacher's Pet Publications, Inc.

Copyright Teacher's Pet Publications 1997
11504 Hammock Point
Berlin MD 21811

Only the student materials in this unit plan (such as worksheets,
study questions, and tests) may be reproduced multiple times
for use in the purchaser's classroom.

For any additional copyright questions,
contact Teacher's Pet Publications.

www.tpet.com

TABLE OF CONTENTS - *Bridge to Terabithia*

Introduction	5
Unit Objectives	8
Reading Assignment Sheet	9
Unit Outline	10
Study Questions (Short Answer)	13
Quiz/Study Questions (Multiple Choice)	23
Pre-reading Vocabulary Worksheets	39
Lesson One (Introductory Lesson)	55
Nonfiction Assignment Sheet	60
Oral Reading Evaluation Form	67
Writing Assignment 1	56
Writing Assignment 2	61
Writing Assignment 3	74
Project	129
Writing Evaluation Form	69
Vocabulary Review Activities	83
Extra Writing Assignments/Discussion ?s	76
Unit Review Activities	85
Unit Tests	89
Unit Resource Materials	125
Vocabulary Resource Materials	143

A FEW NOTES ABOUT THE AUTHOR
Katherine Paterson

PATERSON, Katherine (1932-). Three time Newbery award winning author Katherine Paterson calls herself a gypsy. She has lived in three countries and many states. She doesn't feel she has a home in that sense, so to her, she doesn't have a place out of which stories naturally come.

These sentiments come from an author whose writing in every aspect, not only setting, seems to come very naturally. Characters in Paterson's Newbery Honor book *The Great Gilly Hopkins* and Newbery Medal novels *Jacob Have I Loved* and *Bridge to Terabithia* totally belong where they are. And where they are is where she has spent a good part of her life, in the mid-Atlantic region of the United States. These are her recent works, though. Earlier novels: *The Sign of the Chrysanthemum, Of Nightingales That Weep, and The Master Puppeteer* are set in Japan, where she attended and taught school in the 1950's.

She doesn't think you have to fight dragons to write books, but to live deeply the life you've been given. Her deeply-lived life has taken her all over the world. She spent her early childhood in China, where her father was a missionary. During World War II, she was evacuated with her family. They came to live in various parts of Virginia, North Carolina, and West Virginia, where Katherine's odd clothes and British accent made her an outcast. As a result, she became an avid reader with a vivid imagination.

Katherine feels a book always grows out of who you are. You may wish it to be different, you might even pretend it to be different, but she insists the book will betray you. What you are will always come out in the book, she testifies. When asked what qualifies her to be a writer for children, she responds with the fact the she was once a weird little kid. She thinks that gives her a head start.

Katherine has written a total of twelve books including these most recent: *Lyddie* (1991), *The King's Equal* (1992), and *Flip-Flop Girl* (1994). She and her Presbyterian minister husband, John Paterson, have four children who have provided her with much of the subject matter for her keenly observant stories of family life. She presently lives in Barre, Vermont.

INTRODUCTION

This unit has been designed to develop students' reading, writing, thinking, and language skills through exercises and activities related to *Bridge to Terabithia* by Katherine Paterson. It includes twenty lessons, supported by extra resource materials.

The **introductory lesson** introduces students to one main theme of the novel (friendship) through a bulletin board activity. Following the introductory activity, students are given an explanation of how the activity relates to the book they are about to read. Following the transition, students are given the materials they will be using during the unit.

The **reading assignments** are approximately twenty pages each; some are a little shorter while others are a little longer. Students have approximately 15 minutes of Pre-reading work to do prior to each reading assignment. This Pre-reading work involves reviewing the study questions for the assignment and doing some vocabulary work for 10 vocabulary words they will encounter in their reading.

The **study guide questions** are fact-based questions; students can find the answers to these questions right in the text. These questions come in two formats: short answer or multiple choice. The best use of these materials is probably to use the short answer version of the questions as study guides for students (since answers will be more complete), and to use the multiple choice version for occasional quizzes. If your school has the appropriate machinery, it might be a good idea to make transparencies of your answer keys for the overhead projector.

The **vocabulary work** is intended to enrich students' vocabularies as well as to aid in the students' understanding of the book. Prior to each reading assignment, students will complete a two-part work sheet for 10 vocabulary words in the upcoming reading assignment. Part I focuses on students' use of general knowledge and contextual clues by giving the sentence in which the word appears in the text. Students are then to write down what they think the words mean based on the words' usage. Part II nails down the definitions of the words by giving students dictionary definitions of the words and having students match the words to the correct definitions based on the words' contextual usage. Students should then have an understanding of the words when they meet them in the text.

After each reading assignment, students will go back and formulate answers for the study guide questions. Discussion of these questions serves as a **review** of the most important events and ideas presented in the reading assignments.

After students complete extra discussion questions, there is a **vocabulary review** lesson which pulls together all of the fragmented vocabulary lists for the reading assignments and gives students a review of all of the words they have studied.

Following the reading of the book, two lessons are devoted to the **extra discussion questions/writing assignments/activities**. These questions focus on interpretation, critical analysis and personal response, employing a variety of thinking skills and adding to the students' understanding of the novel. These questions are done as a **group activity**. Using the information they have acquired so far through individual work and class discussions, students get together to further examine the text and to brainstorm ideas relating to the themes of the novel.

The group activity is followed by a **reports and discussion/ activity** session in which the groups share their ideas about the book with the entire class; thus, the entire class gets exposed to many different ideas regarding the themes and events of the book.

There are three **writing assignments** in this unit, each with the purpose of informing, persuading, or having students express personal opinions. The first assignment is to inform: students compose a "want ad" in which they advertise to find a friend. This assignment pulls in the theme of friendship and the skills necessary to write a "want ad." The second assignment gives students the opportunity to express their personal ideas: students will describe their ideal fantasy place and the role they would assume within it. The third assignment is to give students a chance to persuade: students will pretend to be Jesse and try to persuade his parents to allow him to go to a special art school his teacher has arranged.

In addition, there is a **nonfiction reading assignment**. Students are required to read a piece of nonfiction related in some way to *Bridge to Terabithia*. After reading their nonfiction pieces, students will fill out a work sheet on which they answer questions regarding facts, interpretation, criticism, and personal opinions. During one class period, students make **oral presentations** about the nonfiction pieces they have read. This not only exposes all students to a wealth of information, it also gives students the opportunity to practice **public speaking**.

There is an optional **class project** (Build a Bridge) through which students will have the opportunity to act on their interpretation of this passage.

The **review lesson** pulls together all of the aspects of the unit. The teacher is given four or five choices of activities or games to use which all serve the same basic function of reviewing all of the information presented in the unit.

The **unit test** comes in two formats: all multiple choice-matching-true/false or with a mixture of matching, short answer, and composition. As a convenience, two different tests for each format have been included.

There are additional **support materials** included with this unit. The **extra activities** section includes suggestions for an in-class library, crossword and word search puzzles related to the novel, and extra vocabulary games and work sheets. There is a list of **bulletin board ideas** which gives the teacher suggestions for bulletin boards to go along with this unit. In addition, there is a list of **extra class activities** the teacher could choose from to enhance the unit or as a substitution for an exercise the teacher might feel is inappropriate for his/her class. **Answer keys** are located directly after the **reproducible student materials** throughout the unit. The student materials may be reproduced for use in the teacher's classroom without infringement of copyrights. No other portion of this unit may be reproduced without the written consent of Teacher's Pet Publications, Inc.

UNIT OBJECTIVES - *Bridge to Terabithia*

1. Through reading Katherine Paterson's *Bridge to Terabithia*, students will gain an appreciation for the value of friendship and personal growth.

2. Students will be exposed to the trauma of a character dealing with the death of a friend and the stages of grief.

3. Students will define their own viewpoints on the aforementioned themes.

4. Students will gain appreciation for and demonstrate proficiency in identifying and using figurative language.

5. Students will demonstrate their understanding of the text on four levels: factual, interpretive, critical and personal.

6. Students will be given the opportunity to practice reading aloud and silently to improve their skills in each area.

7. Students will answer questions to demonstrate their knowledge and understanding of the main events and characters in *Bridge to Terabithia* as they relate to the author's theme development.

8. Students will enrich their vocabularies and improve their understanding of the novel through the vocabulary lessons prepared for use in conjunction with the novel.

9. The writing assignments in this unit are geared to several purposes:
    a. To have students demonstrate their abilities to inform, to persuade, or to express their own personal ideas
        Note: Students will demonstrate ability to write effectively to <u>inform</u> by developing and organizing facts to convey information. Students will demonstrate the ability to write effectively to <u>persuade</u> by selecting and organizing relevant information, establishing an argumentative purpose, and by designing an appropriate strategy for an identified audience. Students will demonstrate the ability to write effectively to <u>express personal ideas</u> by selecting a form and its appropriate elements.
    b. To check the students' reading comprehension
    c. To make students think about the ideas presented by the novel
    d. To encourage logical thinking
    e. To provide an opportunity to practice good grammar and improve students' use of the English language.

READING ASSIGNMENT SHEET - *Bridge to Terabithia*

Date Assigned	Reading Assignment (Chapters)	Completion Date
	1, 2	
	3, 4	
	5, 6	
	7, 8	
	9, 10, 11	
	12, 13	

UNIT OUTLINE - *Bridge to Terabithia*

1	2	3	4	5
Theme Introduction Writing Assignment 1	Materials PVR Ch. 1,2	Study? Ch. 1,2 PVR Ch. 3,4	Study? Ch. 3,4 PVR Ch. 5,6	Nonfiction Rdg Writing Assignment #2
6	**7**	**8**	**9**	**10**
Study? Ch. 5,6 PVR Ch. 7,8	Figurative Language	Study? Ch. 7, 8 Share Nonfiction PV Ch. 9-11	Read Ch. 9-11 Oral Rdg Evaluation	Finish Rdg Writing Conference
11	**12**	**13**	**14**	**15**
Grief PVR Ch. 12,13	Study? Ch. 12,13 Jesse's Grief	Share "Want Ad" posters Writing Assignment #3	Extra Discussion Questions	Extra Discussion Questions
16	**17**	**18**	**19**	**20**
Extra Discussion/ Activities Sharing Writing Assignments #2, 3	Vocabulary Review	Review	Test	Project Build a Bridge

Key: P = Preview Study Questions   V = Vocabulary Work   R = Read

STUDY GUIDE QUESTIONS

SHORT ANSWER STUDY GUIDE QUESTIONS - *Bridge to Terabithia*

Chapters 1, 2
1. Who is Jesse Oliver Aarons, Jr.?
2. Why does he rise so early in the morning every day during summer vacation?
3. List the daughters in the Aarons' household from oldest to youngest.
4. Why had the lower grade boys started the races during recess?
5. Where did Ellie and Brenda get to go with the Timmons family?
6. Which sister worships Jesse?
7. What is Jesse's favorite pastime?
8. Who is Miss Julia Edmunds and why is she special to Jesse?
9. What kind of relationship do Jesse and his father have?
10. Describe Leslie Burke.

Chapters 3, 4
1. What idea does Jesse have for his drawings during 'down time' the first day back at school?
2. Why do Gary Fulcher and Jesse have a conflict before lunch?
3. Where do the Lark Creek students eat lunch and why?
4. What surprise occurs at recess?
5. When does Jesse finally decide to befriend Leslie?
6. How does Jesse react to Leslie's essay on scuba diving?
7. Why does the class give Leslie a hard time after Mrs. Myers assigns the TV program homework?
8. What surprisingly courageous thing does Jesse do on the bus ride home that afternoon?
9. How does Leslie bribe May Belle so she and Jesse can spend the afternoon by themselves?
10. Where do Jesse and Leslie go and what do they call it?
11. What does Leslie tell Jesse she imagines about their teacher that amuses him?
12. Describe Leslie's parents.
13. How do Jesse's parents feel about his relationship with Leslie?

Chapters 5, 6
1. What did Janice Avery do to May Belle?
2. How do Jesse and Leslie seek revenge?
3. Why does Jesse become angry when Brenda criticizes Leslie?
4. As Christmas nears, Jesse is getting more concerned. Why?
5. How does he solve his problem?
6. What does Leslie give Jesse for Christmas?
7. For what reason is Jesse's dad displeased on Christmas morning?

Short Answer Study Guide Questions - *Bridge to Terabithia* Page 2

Chapters 7, 8
1. Why isn't Leslie around much after Christmas?
2. In what way do Leslie and Jesse feel differently about their parents?
3. Why does Leslie invite Jesse to help her and her dad fix up the house?
4. Explain what the title to chapter seven refers to.
5. Jesse and Leslie go to the pine grove after returning to their kingdom after a month's absence. Why?
6. Something happens to make Jesse and Leslie feel sorry for Janice Avery. What?
7. How do they help her?
8. What Lark Creek Elementary rule had Janice broken?
9. Why was Jesse mad at May Belle at the end of chapter 7?
10. Explain why Ellie and Brenda were upset about the upcoming Easter?
11. Where does Leslie ask Jesse to take her that surprises him?
12. What is the main point of disagreement between May Belle and Leslie on the way home from church?

Chapters 9-11
1. How did Jesse react when he and Leslie went to the swollen creek bed on Easter Monday?
2. On Wednesday why did Leslie think some evil being had put a curse on their beloved kingdom?
3. Why did Jesse awake with a feeling of dread Wednesday night?
4. Why had Miss Edmunds called Jesse?
5. After Miss Edmunds picked Jesse up, what does he realize he could have done?
6. Give Jesse's reaction upon entering the National Art Gallery?
7. Which display in the Smithsonian is Jesse attracted to the most? Why?
8. Jesse's father delivers shocking news when Jesse returns from Washington? What is it?
9. What does Jesse do after he is told about Leslie?
10. When Jesse awakens in the middle of the night, how does he push away the falling sensation?
11. Why does Brenda continue to question Jesse at breakfast Friday morning?

Short Answer Study Guide Questions - *Bridge to Terabithia* Page 3

Chapters 12, 13
1. Describe the scene at the Burke's house Friday morning.
2. Why does Jesse become angry while there? What does he do?
3. Where does he go and for what?
4. What does Jesse's father say to him that makes him feel like he's being treated like a man?
5. After milking Bessie Saturday morning where does Jesse go and why?
6. Who shows up and what problem does she face?
7. How does Jesse help her?
8. Why does Jesse think Mrs. Myers sends him out in the hall?
9. What does she say to him that comes as a surprise?
10. When the Burkes return from Pennsylvania what do they do?
11. How does Jesse use the leftover lumber from the Burkes?
12. What role does May Belle assume at the end of the book?

ANSWER KEY: SHORT ANSWER STUDY GUIDE QUESTIONS
Bridge to Terabithia

Chapters 1, 2

1. Who is Jesse Oliver Aarons, Jr.?
    A long-legged ten-year-old boy in a family of all girls living in a Northern Virginia rural area.

2. Why does he rise so early in the morning every day during summer vacation?
    He gets up to practice running so he can be the fastest boy in fifth grade when school resumes.

3. List the daughters in the Aarons' household from oldest to youngest.
    Ellie, Brenda, May Belle, and Joyce Ann.

4. Why had the lower grade boys started the races during recess?
    They started the races because the older kids hogged up all the good equipment or field space.

5. Where did Ellie and Brenda get to go with the Timmons family?
    The girls went school shopping to the Millsburg Plaza.

6. Which sister worships Jesse?
    Jesse's six-year-old sister, May Belle, worships him.

7. What is Jesse's favorite pastime?
    Jesse draws the way some people drink.

8. Who is Miss Julia Edmunds and why is she special to Jesse?
    She is the denim-clad hippie-type music teacher who thinks Jesse is unusually talented.

9. What kind of relationship do Jesse and his father have?
    Jesse longs for a closer relationship with his father who is gone from sun-up to late every night working in Washington.

10. Describe Leslie Burke.
    Jesse can't decide if the person is a girl or a boy. She has dark short-cropped hair and dresses in pants.

Chapters 3, 4

1. What idea does Jesse have for his drawings during 'down time' the first day back at school?
    He wants to do a whole book of drawings with one chief animal character.

2. Why do Gary Fulcher and Jesse have a conflict before lunch?
    Gary tries to yank Jesse's drawing away from him and Jesse stomps on his foot.

3. Where do the Lark Creek students eat lunch and why?
    They must eat lunch at their seats because they have no lunchroom.

4. What surprise occurs at recess?
    Leslie wants to run with the boys, which is unheard of at their school, **and** she beats them.

5. When does Jesse finally decide to befriend Leslie?
    Jesse is feeling delighted during Miss Edmunds' music class while they all sit on the floor. He decides to smile at Leslie and she smiles back.

6. How does Jesse react to Leslie's essay on scuba diving?
    He is so strongly affected he feels like he is drowning.

7. Why does the class give Leslie a hard time after Mrs. Myers assigns the TV program for homework?
    She admits to the teacher that her family has no TV.

8. What surprisingly courageous thing does Jesse do on the bus ride home that afternoon?
    He retrieves Leslie from the back of the bus where Janice Avery always sits and makes a rude comment to Janice on her way back to her seat so she won't pick on Leslie.

9. How does Leslie bribe May Belle so she and Jesse can spend the afternoon by themselves?
    She gives her a brand new, never-been- opened package of paper dolls to take home and punch out to play with.

10. Where do Jesse and Leslie go and what do they call it?
    They find a rope hanging from a crab apple tree that swings across a creek bed. The creek bed separates the farmland from the woods. They decide to make a secret place, just for the two of them, just a few yards beyond the creek bed and swing. They call it Terabithia.

11. What does Leslie tell Jesse she imagines about their teacher that amuses him?
    Leslie imagines funny stories about their teacher during class, like her at a fat farm, and relates the details to Jesse at recess.

12. Describe Leslie's parents.
    They are young, with straight white teeth, and lots of hair. Leslie calls them by their first names which bothers Jesse. They wear designer jeans and talk about intellectual things. They are both writers.

13. How do Jesse's parents feel about his relationship with Leslie?
    They are worried that their only son does nothing but play with girls and they worry about what will become of him.

Chapters 5, 6

1. What did Janice Avery do to May Belle?
   She stole May Belle's Twinkies.

2. How do Jesse and Leslie seek revenge?
   They plant a note in her desk supposedly written by a popular seventh grade boy professing his undying love for her and asking her to meet him after school

3. Why does Jesse become angry when Brenda criticizes Leslie?
   He can't believe he is related to someone he thinks is as dumb as Brenda and that she would dare criticize Leslie, whom he respects more.

4. As Christmas nears, Jesse is getting more concerned. Why?
   He doesn't have a Christmas present for Leslie yet.

5. How does he solve his problem?
   He sees a sign for free puppies while riding home on the bus and decides to hop off and get one for her.

6. What does Leslie give Jesse for Christmas?
   She gives him a box of watercolors with twenty-four tubes of color, three brushes, and a pad of heavy art paper.

7. For what reason is Jesse's dad displeased on Christmas morning?
   The electric racing-car set he bought for Jesse wasn't working properly. The cars kept coming off the track at the curves.

Chapters 7, 8

1. Why isn't Leslie around much after Christmas?
    She is helping her dad fix-up the house.

2. In what way do Leslie and Jesse feel differently about their parents?
    Leslie likes to relate to her parents: to understand them; while Jesse thinks parents are what they are, not something for you to try to puzzle out. He thinks there is something weird about a grown man wanting to be friends with his own child.

3. Why does Leslie invite Jesse to help her and her dad fix up the house?
    She realizes Jesse is unhappy about her spending all her time with her dad, so she tells him he could offer to help too.

4. Explain what the title to chapter seven refers to.
    They painted the room they were working on gold. It was an enchanting sight to behold with the sun streaming in from the west.

5. Jesse and Leslie go to the pine grove after returning to their kingdom after a month's absence. Why?
    They go to the sacred place to give thanks for their victory against the imaginary foe they defeated upon their return to their kingdom.

6. Something happens to make Jesse and Leslie feel sorry for Janice Avery. What?
    Leslie overhears her crying in the girls' bathroom.

7. How do they help her?
    Jesse insists they need to try to help her. Leslie is opposed but agrees to go into the girls' bathroom and try to talk to her.

8. What Lark Creek Elementary rule had Janice broken?
    You never mix up troubles at home with life at school. By admitting her father was beating her, it was viewed that she had betrayed him.

9. Why was Jesse mad at May Belle at the end of chapter 7?
    She had followed him to Terabithia and he was afraid she would squeal to their mother about their secret place.

10. Explain why Ellie and Brenda were upset about the upcoming Easter?
    Their father had been laid off and they could not get anything new to wear to church.

11. Where does Leslie ask Jesse to take her that surprises him?
    She has never been to church and asks to go along for Easter.

12. What is the main point of disagreement between May Belle and Leslie on the way home from church?
    May Belle says that God will damn you to hell when you die if you don't believe in the Bible. Leslie disagrees.

Chapters 9-11

1. How did Jesse react when he and Leslie went to the swollen creek bed on Monday?
   He was awed by the scene of the swift water rushing and thought they ought to forget going across.

2. On Wednesday why did Leslie think some evil being had put a curse on their beloved kingdom?
   While they were sitting in the castle, it began suddenly to rain so hard that the water came through the top of the shack in icy streams.

3. Why did Jesse awake with a feeling of dread Wednesday night?
   It was still raining and he knew he had to tell Leslie he wouldn't go to Terabithia. He didn't mind telling her as much as he minded being afraid to go.

4. Why had Miss Edmunds called Jesse?
   She invited him to go to Washington D. C. to go to the National Art Gallery and the Smithsonian.

5. After Miss Edmunds picked Jesse up, what does he realize he could have done?
   He realizes he could have invited Leslie to come along, but actually he is thrilled to be spending the day alone with Miss Edmunds.

6. Give Jesse's reaction upon entering the National Art Gallery?
   It was like stepping into the pine grove- the huge vaulted marble, the cool splash of the fountain, and the green glowing all around. He felt drunk with the color, form, and hugeness.

7. Which display in the Smithsonian is Jesse attracted to the most? Why?
   He is attracted to the display of the miniature scene of Indians disguised in buffalo skins scaring a herd of buffalo over a cliff to their death. It was a three-dimensional nightmare version of some of his own drawings. He felt a sense of kinship.

8. Jesse's father delivers shocking news when Jesse returns from Washington? What is it?
    His father tells him they found the Burke girl down in the creek, drowned.

9. What does Jesse do after he is told about Leslie?
    He yells that they are lying to him and runs out the door away from everything.

10. When Jesse awakens in the middle of the night, how does he push away the falling sensation?
    He puts his mind to recalling the day in Washington, working on details of pictures and statues, dredging up the sound of Miss Edmunds' voice, recalling his own exact words and her exact answers.

11. Why does Brenda continue to question Jesse at breakfast Friday morning?
    She can't believe he is sitting there gobbling down plates of pancakes instead of reacting to Leslie's death. He is in denial.

Chapters 12, 13

1. Describe the scene at the Burke's house Friday morning.
    Four or five people Jesse had never seen before were sitting about. Leslie's grandmother acknowledges Jesse and his parents. Her dad hugs Jesse tightly and sobs while talking to Jesse.

2. Why does Jesse become angry while there? What does he do?
    When her dad tells Jesse she has been cremated he realizes he will never see her again and he is furious. He thinks they are all crying for themselves, not Leslie. He is mad enough to sock her dad, but runs off towards home. Upon reaching home, he hits May Belle in the face after she asks if he saw her laid out.

3. Where does Jesse go and for what?
    He retrieves the paints and paper Leslie had given him for Christmas from under his mattress, takes them down to the stream and flings them into the dirty brown water.

4. What does Jesse's father say to him that makes him feel like he's being treated like a man?
    His father follows him and sits down next to him on the dirt and pulls him onto his lap. He says, "Hell, ain't it?"

5. After milking Bessie Saturday morning where does Jesse go and why?
    He goes to the stream and finds a large tree branch that has washed up into the bank. He uses it to cross over into Terabithia. He then makes a funeral wreath out of a pine bough bent into a circle adorned with spring beauties from the forest floor. He and P. T. take it to the sacred pine grove and lay it on the thick carpet of golden needles and Jesse says : "Father, into Thy hands I commend her spirit." He felt Leslie would have approved of the words for they had the ring of the sacred grove in them.

6. Who shows up and what problem does she face?
    May Belle follows Jesse and is halfway across the tree bridge. She is terrified to move forwards or backwards.

7. How does Jesse help her?
    He inches out on the branch until he is close enough to touch her. He then tells her to back up and holding onto her, he guides her backwards to the home side of the bank.

8. Why does Jesse think Mrs. Myers sends him out in the hall?
    He did not stand up for the morning pledge to the flag.

9. What does she say to him that comes as a surprise?
    She wants to give him her sympathy. She shares her grief over the loss of her husband and tells him she knows how hard it must be for him. She suggests they try to help each other.

10. When the Burkes return from Pennsylvania what do they do?
    They have a U-haul truck and plan to leave now that Leslie is gone. Jess and his dad help them pack it and his mother brings down sandwiches.

11. How does Jesse use the leftover lumber from the Burkes?
    He builds a sturdy bridge over the creek to Terabithia.

12. What role does May Belle assume at the end of the book?
    Jesse puts flowers in her hair and leads her across the bridge to the kingdom telling her the kingdom has been waiting for a new queen.

MULTIPLE CHOICE STUDY GUIDE/QUIZ QUESTIONS- *Bridge to Terabithia*

Chapters 1, 2

1. Jesse Oliver Aarons is
    a. a young girl from Washington D. C. who moves to Virginia.
    b. a ten-year-old boy in a family of all sisters.
    c. the fastest runner in third grade at Lark Creek Elementary.
    d. none of the above

2. Jesse rises extra early every day of summer vacation because
    a. he wants to improve his running time for the next school year.
    b. it is the only free time he has away from all his brothers and sisters.
    c. he hates sharing his room with two girls and gets up to sleep in the barn with the cow.
    d. he has to milk the family cow before anyone else arises.

3. Select the correct list of girls in Jesse's family going from eldest to youngest.
    a. Brenda, Ellie, Joyce Ann, May Belle
    b. Jessie, Joyce Ann, Brenda, Ellie
    c. Ellie, Leslie, Brenda, May Belle.
    d. Ellie, Brenda, May Belle, Joyce Ann.

4. The lower grade boys had started the races during recess because
    a. the older boys took the dry center of the upper field for their ball games.
    b. all the balls went to the upper grades.
    c. the girls claimed the small top section for hopscotch or jump rope.
    d. all of the above

5. Ellie and Brenda went
    a. school shopping with their mother.
    b. to the local swimming pool with the neighbors.
    c. shopping to Millsburg Plaza with the Timmons family.
    d. roller skating with their boyfriends.

6. Which sister of Jessie's worships him?
    a. May Belle
    b. Brenda
    c. Joyce Ann
    d. Ellie

Study Guide/Quiz Questions- *Bridge to Terabithia* Multiple Choice Format Page 2

7. Jesse's favorite pastime is
    a. fishing.
    b. drawing.
    c. running.
    d. writing.

8. Miss Julia Edmunds is
    a. the itinerant art teacher at Lark Creek.
    b. Lark Creek Elementary's music teacher.
    c. a teacher who thinks Jesse is unusually talented
    d. both b and c

9. Jesse and his father
    a. work together and are very close.
    b. don't see much of each other.
    c. fight about Jessie's chores.
    d. spend hours fishing and talking over the weekends.

10. Leslie Burke is
    a. a young girl with short, dark hair who looks like a boy.
    b. a friend of Jesse's sister, Ellie.
    c. a new neighbor who just moved into the old Smith house.
    d. May Belle's new doll.

SStudy Guide/Quiz Questions- *Bridge to Terabithia* Multiple Choice Format Page 3

Chapters 3, 4

1. During 'down-time' at school the first day, Jesse decides he will
    a. make a book of his drawings with one chief animal character.
    b. never become friends with Leslie Burke.
    c. keep his distance from the troublemaker, Gary Fulcher.
    d. not run in the lunchtime recess races.

2. Gary Fulcher and Jesse have a conflict before lunch over
    a. who will run first in the races.
    b. Jesse's drawings.
    c. the most popular girl in fifth grade.
    d. who was to hand out the books for the teacher.

3. Lark Creek Elementary students eat lunch
    a. in the cafeteria with the teachers.
    b. outside when the weather is nice.
    c. at their desks because there is no official lunchroom.
    d. at home because all the students live close enough to walk to school.

4. The big surprise at recess is
    a. The lower field is too muddy to run on due to the recent storm.
    b. The older boys are now racing each other.
    c. The gym teacher won't let the boys race because it is too close to physical education time.
    d. Leslie insists on running with the boys and beats them all.

5. Jesse finally decides to befriend Leslie when
    a. she keeps bugging him about it.
    b. they are on the bus and he no longer wants to sit with May Belle.
    c. they are in music class and he is in a delightful mood.
    d. she shows up in the barn to help him milk the cow.

6. Mrs. Myers reads Leslie's essay on scuba diving to the class. What is Jesse's reaction?
    a. He feels sorry for her because the other good writers will snub her.
    b. He is jealous because no one around there has a hobby such as that.
    c. He is enthralled with it and feels as if he is drowning.
    d. He tells her to stop trying to be such a teacher's pet.

Study Guide/Quiz Questions- *Bridge to Terabithia* Multiple Choice Format Page 4

7. The class harasses Leslie because
    a. she has no TV set to watch the Jacques Cousteau special.
    b. they are sick of Mrs. Myers giving her all the recognition.
    c. she is different than they are and looks like a boy.
    d. none of the above

8. Jesse backs down to the seventh-grade bully, Janice Avery, that day on the bus ride home.
    a. true
    b. false

9. Leslie bribes May Belle so she and Jesse can spend the afternoon by themselves by giving her
    a. a baby doll that walks and talks.
    b. a pad of paper and a new box of crayons.
    c. some of her favorite candy.
    d. a brand new package of paper dolls.

10. Where do Jesse and Leslie go?
    a. They go back to the schoolyard and practice running against each other.
    b. They go over the creek bed on a rope swing and claim the land as their secret place.
    c. They go to the barn and Jesse shows Leslie how to milk Bessie.
    d. They run to her house and she shows him all of her expensive toys.

11. Leslie imagines funny stories about their teacher during class and tells Jesse at recess.
    a. true
    b. false

12. Leslie's parents are
    a. highly educated.
    b. writers in designer jeans.
    c. straight- teethed and have lots of hair.
    d. all of the above

13. Jesse's parents worry what will happen to him because
    a. he spends all his time with a girl.
    b. he spends too much time fishing.
    c. he isn't doing well in school.
    d. he isn't doing the chores he is supposed to do.

Study Guide/Quiz Questions- *Bridge to Terabithia* Multiple Choice Format Page 5

Chapters 5,6

1. Janice Avery stole
    a. Jesse's drawings.
    b. Leslie's paint set and paper.
    c. May Belle's Twinkie
    d. Brenda's boyfriend.

2. Jesse and Leslie seek revenge by
    a. beating Janice up on the bus.
    b. telling the principal what she did.
    c. fooling her into believing a popular boy loved her.
    d. leaving her a note with gossip about her friends.

3. When Brenda criticizes Leslie, Jesse
    a. smacks her in the face.
    b. becomes angry because he thinks more of Leslie that his own sister.
    c. tells their mother on her.
    d. throws his breakfast dish at her.

4. Jesse's biggest problem before Christmas is
    a. he has no gift for Leslie.
    b. lack of money to buy May Belle's Barbie doll.
    c. how to tell Leslie he can't afford a gift for her.
    d. all of the above

5. He solves his problem by
    a. combining his money with Ellie's to get May Belle her Barbie.
    b. getting a part time job for the weeks between Thanksgiving and Christmas.
    c. going away on Christmas to his aunt and uncle's.
    d. giving Leslie a free puppy.

6. For Christmas Leslie gives Jesse
    a. watercolors
    b. brushes
    c. a pad of thick art paper
    d. all of the above

7. Jesse's dad is unhappy on Christmas morning because
    a. the racing-car track isn't running properly.
    b. Jesse doesn't like his gift.
    c. the girls will not quit bickering.
    d. he couldn't afford to buy his children more expensive gifts for Christmas.

Study Guide/Quiz Questions- *Bridge to Terabithia* Multiple Choice Format Page 7

Chapters 7, 8

1. Leslie isn't around much after Christmas because
    a. she is visiting her grandparents in Pennsylvania.
    b. she is helping her dad fix-up the house.
    c. she went to Arlington to visit some of her old friends.
    d. she and her mother are working around the house.

2. Leslie and Jesse feel differently about their parents. She feels parents are not to be understood, just accepted. He wants to be friends with his parents.
    a. true
    b. false

3. Leslie invites Jessie to
    a. help her and her father restore the house.
    b. come to Pennsylvania to visit her grandparents with her.
    c. go to Arlington to visit a friend.
    d. come to a New Year's dinner.

4. "The Golden Room" is a good name for chapter seven because
    a. the chapter is all about the myth of the goose and the golden egg.
    b. they couldn't decide whether to paint the room blue or gold.
    c. the chapter is about fixing-up the room they paint gold.
    d. they find gold beneath the old, black floor boards.

5. Jess and Leslie go to the pine grove after returning to their kingdom to
    a. see if anything had changed.
    b. say the blessing of the pines.
    c. give thanks for their victory against the imaginary foe they defeated.
    d. look for a lost doe.

6. What makes Jesse feel sorry for Janice Avery?
    a. Leslie reports she overheard her crying in the girls' bathroom.
    b. She has lost her best friend.
    c. Her family deserted her.
    d. She is failing seventh grade.

Study Guide/Quiz Questions- *Bridge to Terabithia* Multiple Choice Format Page 8

7. Jesse and Leslie help Janice Avery by
    a. taking her note to the boy she liked.
    b. beating up her friends.
    c. telling the teacher the nature of her problems.
    d. approaching her and listening to her problems.

8. Janice Avery broke this rule:
    a. do unto others as you would have others do unto you.
    b. never tell someone you don't trust a secret.
    c. never mix up troubles from home with life at school.
    d. be friendly; all else will follow.

9. Jesse is upset with May Belle because
    a. she is acting like one of the older sisters.
    b. he doesn't want to share Leslie with her.
    c. she won't stay away from his paints and paper.
    d. she followed him and she may tell their parents about the secret place.

10. Ellie and Brenda are upset because
    a. their dad got laid off.
    b. they won't get anything new to wear to Easter Sunday service.
    c. Jesse has a rich friend who buys him nice things.
    d. their boyfriends dumped them right before the spring dance.

11. Where does Leslie ask to go that surprises Jesse?
    a. museum
    b. farm convention
    c. Millsburg
    d. church

12. Leslie and May Belle disagree about
    a. the church service they just left.
    b. Jesus dying on the cross.
    c. reading the Bible in a year.
    d. God damning to hell those that do not believe.

Study Guide/Quiz Questions- *Bridge to Terabithia* Multiple Choice Format Page 9

Chapters 9-11

1. When Jesse sees the swollen creek bed on Monday he
    a. is awed by the sound and size of the creek.
    b. doesn't want to swing over on the rope to the other side.
    c. is fearful.
    d. all of the above

2. Why did Leslie think some evil being had put a curse on their beloved kingdom?
    a. they could hear eerie noises coming from the castle.
    b. the rain came through the top of their castle in icy streams.
    c. the rain had washed their castle away.
    d. none of the above

3. Jesse awoke with a feeling of dread Wednesday night due to
    a. the unending rain.
    b. the fact that he is afraid to re-enter Terabithia while the creek is swollen.
    c. he knows he must tell Leslie he won't go.
    d. all of the above

4. Miss Edmunds calls Jesse to see if he wants to learn how to play the guitar, since it was still raining.
    a. true
    b. false

5. Jesse realized he could have
    a. invited Leslie to go along.
    b. fully wakened his mother and told her where he went so she wouldn't worry.
    c. tried to reach his father.
    d. left a note for his mother.

6. Jesse's reaction upon entering the National Art Gallery was one of
    a. fear of all the crowds.
    b. drunkenness with the color, form, and hugeness.
    c. doubt of the authenticity of the art.
    d. none of the above

Study Guide/Quiz Questions- *Bridge to Terabithia* Multiple Choice Format Page 10

7. Jesse is most attracted to which display in the Smithsonian?
    a. the dinosaur
    b. the tunnel-makers
    c. the Indians and buffalo
    d. the First Ladies' gowns

8. When Jesse returns from Washington, his father tells him
    a. they thought he was dead because no one knew where he was.
    b. Miss Edmunds can not take students from their homes without written permission.
    c. Leslie has drowned in the swollen creek.
    d. the rope to their secret place is in bad shape.

9. After hearing the bad news Jesse
    a. runs out of the house calling them liars.
    b. goes to his room and flops on the bed.
    c. tunes everyone out and asks for supper.
    d. runs to the rope swing to see for himself.

10. When Jesse awakens in the middle of the night, he pushes away the falling sensation by
    a. reciting the Lord's Prayer.
    b. recalling and reciting the past day's events with Miss Edmunds, detail by detail.
    c. remembering everything Leslie ever told him.
    d. counting sheep.

11. Brenda is upset with Jesse because he
    a. acts like he doesn't care about Leslie's death.
    b. is in denial.
    c. eats a couple of plates of pancakes.
    d. all of the above

Chapters 12, 13

1. Jesse knew everyone at the Burke's house when he and his parents went to pay their respects.
    a. true
    b. false

2. Why does Jesse hit May Belle in the face?
    a. He was angry Leslie had been cremated.
    b. She was in his paints again.
    c. She asked the wrong thing at the wrong time.
    d. both a and c

3. What does he do after he retrieves his paints and paper Leslie had given him?
    a. He burns them in the garbage pile.
    b. He flings them in the swollen stream.
    c. He gives them to May Belle.
    d. He gives them back to Leslie's parents.

4. What does Jesse's father say to him that makes him feel like he's being treated like a man?
    a. "Hell, ain't it?"
    b. "That was a damn fool thing to do."
    c. "Life's not easy, son."
    d. "Men don't cry."

5. After milking Bessie Saturday morning where does Jesse go and why?
    a. He goes back to the old Perkins place to see what has been left.
    b. He goes straight to the pine grove to offer Leslie's spirits to the gods.
    c. He goes to Terabithia to make a pine bough funeral wreath; then takes it to the pine grove.
    d. He goes to the nearest stream and watches it thinking about Leslie's death.

6. Who shows up and what problem does she face?
    a. Ellie is curious about where he has gone. She wants to talk about their parents.
    b. Leslie's spirit appears to him and she doesn't know how to apologize for leaving him.
    c. Janice Avery has found out about the secret place and wants to take Leslie's place.
    d. May Belle follows Jesse and is halfway across the tree bridge.

7. Jessie is able to help her successfully.
    a. true
    b. false

Study Guide/Quiz Questions- *Bridge to Terabithia* Multiple Choice Format Page 12

8. Mrs. Myers calls Jesse into the hall because
    a. he didn't stand for the pledge of allegiance.
    b. she wants to express her sympathy to him over Leslie's death.
    c. she wants to share with him about her husband and son's deaths.
    d. he threw a tantrum about Leslie's seat being removed before he could touch it.

9. What does she say to him that comes as a surprise?
    a. She knows how much it must hurt him and maybe they can help each other through it.
    b. She thinks he should go home and take the day off.
    c. She doesn't want the other students to know how much she is hurting.
    d. She never taught such a student as Leslie in all her years of teaching.

10. When the Burkes return from Pennsylvania they
    a. sprinkle Leslie's ashes over the stream leading to Terabithia.
    b. give Jesse the urn of ashes for him to do with what he thinks best.
    c. load up their U-Haul and go back to Washington.
    d. tear down the old house and burn the remains in anger and grief.

11. Jesse uses the leftover lumber from the Burkes to
    a. build May Belle a treehouse so she can get away from the rest of the sisters.
    b. chop up into pieces to burn as a sacrifice for Leslie.
    c. construct a better structure to serve as the castle of Terabithia.
    d. build a sturdy bridge over the stream to Terabithia.

12. May Belle now assumes the role of
    a. princess of the pine grove.
    b. queen of Terabithia.
    c. court jester of the kingdom.
    d. queen of the sacred place.

ANSWER KEY- MULTIPLE CHOICE STUDY/QUIZ QUESTIONS
Bridge to Terabithia

Chapters 1, 2
1. B
2. A
3. D
4. D
5. C
6. A
7. B
8. D
9. B
10. A

Chapters 3, 4
1. A
2. B
3. C
4. D
5. C
6. C
7. A
8. B
9. D
10. B
11. A
12. D
13. A

Chapters 5, 6
1. C
2. C
3. B
4. A
5. D
6. D
7. A

Chapters 7, 8
1. B
2. B
3. A
4. C
5. C
6. A
7. D
8. C
9. D
10. B
11. D
12. D

Chapters 9-11
1. D
2. B
3. D
4. B
5. A
6. B
7. C
8. C
9. A
10. B
11. D

Chapters 12, 13
1. B
2. D
3. B
4. A
5. C
6. D
7. A
8. B
9. A
10. C
11. D
12. B

PREREADING VOCABULARY WORKSHEETS

Vocabulary - *Bridge to Terabithia*

<u>Chapters 1-2</u> **Part I:** Using Prior Knowledge and Contextual Clues
Below are the sentences in which the vocabulary words appear in the text. Read the sentence. Use any clues you can find in the sentence combined with your prior knowledge, and write what you think the underlined words mean on the lines provided.

1. He had never learned to run properly, but he was long-legged for a ten-year-old, and no one had more *grit* than he.

   _____

2. Not just for the first heat but the whole *shebang*.

   _____

3. Brenda pinched her nose with her pinky crooked *delicately*.

   _____

4. Jess made peanut-butter sandwiches for the little girls and himself, and because the kitchen was still hot and almost *nauseatingly* full of bean smell, the three of them went outside to eat.

   _____

5. Then her *pudgy* body shuddered and she let out great cry.

   _____

6. The peace would start at the top of his *muddled* brain and seep down through his tired and tensed-up body.

   _____

7. So the students of Lark Creek Elementary sat at their desks all Friday, their hearts thumping with anticipation as they listened to the joyful *pandemonium* pouring out from the teachers' room.

   _____

Bridge to Terabithia Vocabulary Chapters 1-2 Continued

8. It wouldn't help to try to defend Miss Edmunds against their unjust and *hypocritical* attacks.

_____

9. "You're the *proverbial* diamond in the rough," she'd said to him once, touching his nose lightly with the tip of her electrifying finger.

_____

10. His dad would be home soon, and so would those <u>cagey</u> girls who managed somehow to have all the fun and leave him and their mother with all the work.

_____

Part II: Determining the Meaning   Match the vocabulary words to their dictionary definitions.

___ 1. grit   A. sly; tricky
___ 2. shebang   B. obvious; proven
___ 3. delicately   C. backbone
___ 4. nauseatingly   D. in a sissified manner
___ 5. pudgy   E. sickeningly
___ 6. muddled   F. confused
___ 7. pandemonium   G. the whole thing
___ 8. hypocritical   H. uproar
___ 9. proverbial   I. chubby
___10. cagey   J. two-faced

Vocabulary - *Bridge to Terabithia* Chapters 3-4

Part I: Using Prior Knowledge and Contextual Clues
Below are the sentences in which the vocabulary words appear in the text. Read the sentence. Use any clues you can find in the sentence combined with your prior knowledge, and write what you think the underlined words mean on the lines provided.

11. Jess now knew that he would never be the best runner of the fourth and fifth grades, and his only *consolation* was that neither would Gray Fulcher.

___

12. He felt there in the teachers' room that it was the beginning of a new season in his life, and he chose *deliberately* to make it so.

___

13. She was quiet for a moment, thinking, Jess decided, about her former school, which he saw as bright and new with a gleaming gymnasium larger than the one at the *consolidated* high school.

___

14. "What if"-Leslie's voice *faltered*, then she shook her head and cleared her throat so the words came out stronger- "what if you don't have a television set?"

___

15. Her Leslie smile shifted suddenly and *ominously* into a scowl that silenced the storm.

___

16. Leslie called to him. *Intoxicated* as he was with the heavens, he couldn't imagine needing anything on earth.

___

17. When Leslie spoke, the words rolling out so *regally*, you knew she was a proper queen.

___

Bridge to Terabithia Vocabulary Chapters 3-4 Continued

18. Between the two of them they owned the world and no enemy, Gary Fulcher, Wanda Kay Moore, Janice Avery, Jess's own fears and *insufficiencies*, nor any of the foes whom Leslie imagined attacking Terabithia, could ever really defeat them.

_____

19. He grabbed the end of the rope and swung out toward the other bank with a kind of wild *exhilaration* and landed gently on his feet, taller, and stronger and wiser in that mysterious land.

_____

20. He nodded, and without speaking, they went back to the creek bank where they shared together a *solemn* meal of crackers and dried fruit.

_____

Part II: Determining the Meaning   Match the vocabulary words to their dictionary definitions.

___ 11. consolation   A. weaknesses
___ 12. deliberately   B. serious
___ 13. consolidated   C. thrill
___ 14. faltered   D. hesitated; wavered
___ 15. ominously   E. comfort
___ 16. intoxicated   F. combined
___ 17. regally   G. drunk
___ 18. insufficiencies   H. threateningly; darkly
___ 19. exhilaration   I. on purpose; intentionally
___ 20. solemn   J. stately; dignified

Vocabulary - *Bridge to Terabithia* Chapters 5-6

Part I: Using Prior Knowledge and Contextual Clues
Below are the sentences in which the vocabulary words appear in the text. Read the sentence. Use any clues you can find in the sentence combined with your prior knowledge, and write what you think the underlined words mean on the lines provided.

21. "Shhh," Leslie said, stroking May Belle's head, but May Belle didn't want comfort, she wanted *revenge*.

_____

22. He nodded *vigorously*. Anything was better than promising to fight Janice Avery.

_____

23. "Hey, girl, you kill the king of Terabithia, and you're in trouble." "*Regicide*," she said proudly.

_____

24. In his head he drew the shadowy castle with the tortured prince pacing the *parapets.*

_____

25. Wilma's face was *crimson* as she screamed out the window, "OK, you dummy! You talk to Willard. You'll see. Just ask him about that letter! You'll see!"

_____

26. This year Ellie and Brenda both had boyfriends at the consolidated high school and the problem of what to give them and what to expect from them was cause of endless *speculation* and fights.

_____

Bridge to Terabithia Vocabulary Chapters 5-6 Continued

27. Fights, because as usual, their mother was complaining that there was hardly enough money to give the little girls something from Santa Claus, let alone a *surplus* to buy record albums or shirts for a pair of boys she'd never set eyes on.

_____

28. Maybe, he thought, I was a *foundling*, like in the stories.

_____

29. By the last week of school before the holiday, he was growing *desperate*.

_____

30. It would have been easier, but he couldn't escape the feeling that one must enter Terabithia only by the *prescribed* entrance.

_____

Part II: Determining the Meaning   Match the vocabulary words to their dictionary definitions.

___ 21. revenge   A. abandoned infant
___ 22. vigorously   B. extra amount; excess
___ 23. regicide   C. to get back at
___ 24. parapets   D. assigned; designated
___ 25. crimson   E. consideration; thought
___ 26. speculation   F. the killing of a king
___ 27. surplus   G. energetically
___ 28. foundling   H. barriers
___ 29. desperate   I. deep red
___ 30. prescribed   J. hopeless

Vocabulary - *Bridge to Terabithia* Chapters 7-8

Part I: Using Prior Knowledge and Contextual Clues
Below are the sentences in which the vocabulary words appear in the text. Read the sentence. Use any clues you can find in the sentence combined with your prior knowledge, and write what you think the underlined words mean on the lines provided.

31. For all his smartness with politics and music, Mr. Burke was *inclined* to be absent-minded.

_____

32. He was afraid he would destroy everything by trying to force the magic on his own, when it was plain that the magic was *reluctant* to come for him.

_____

33. Or maybe it was the time of year- the last *dregs* of winter spoiling the taste of everything.

_____

34. Next they got the old wallpaper off the livingroom wall- all five *garish* layers of it.

_____

35. He crept down the hall after her and hid behind the nearest *alcove* to the girls' room door.

_____

36. "And those two-two-" She looked for a word *vile* enough to describe Janice Avery's friends and found none.

_____

37. Jess was glad to escape to the shed and the *complacent* company of Miss Bessie.

_____

38. " It would make you throw up to see how those girls make a *spectacle* of themselves in church."

_____

Bridge to Terabithia Vocabulary Chapters 7-8 Continued

39. "I'd be *obliged* if you'd finish milking and come on back to the house.

_____

40. Because he wasn't listening to the words, the man's red face with sweat poring down seemed strangely out of place in the dull *sanctuary*.

_____

Part II: Determining the Meaning   Match the vocabulary words to their dictionary definitions.

___ 31. inclined
___ 32. reluctant
___ 33. dregs
___ 34. garish
___ 35. alcove
___ 36. vile
___ 37. complacent
___ 38. spectacle
___ 39. obliged
___ 40. sanctuary

A. remains
B. self-satisfied
C. place of worship
D. unwilling
E. mean; disgusting
F. glaring; ornate
G. recessed opening
H. known to; tendency
I. grateful
J. public display

Vocabulary - *Bridge to Terabithia* Chapters 9-11

Part I: Using Prior Knowledge and Contextual Clues
Below are the sentences in which the vocabulary words appear in the text. Read the sentence. Use any clues you can find in the sentence combined with your prior knowledge, and write what you think the underlined words mean on the lines provided.

41. On Easter Monday the rain began again in earnest. It was as though the elements were *conspiring* to ruin their short week of freedom.

_____

42. The rain continued *sporadically,* so that by Wednesday the creek had swollen to the trunk of the crab apple and they were running through ankle-deep water to make their flight into Terabithia.

_____

43. In the dim light he could see Leslie's face freeze into its most queenly pose- the kind of expression she usually reserved for *vanquished* enemies.

_____

44. He instantly *repented* his unkingly manner.

_____

45. Give us, we beseech thee, wisdom to *discern* this evil, and power to overcome it."

_____

46. "That old rope you kids been swinging on broke." His father went quietly and *relentlessly* on.

_____

47. He could only remember the mood of *dread* it had brought with it.

_____

Bridge to Terabithia Vocabulary Chapters 9-11 Continued

48. He put his mind to remembering the day in Washington, working on details of pictures and statues, *dredging* up the sound of Miss Edmunds' voice, recalling his own exact words and her exact answers.

_____

49. She kept nodding her head. "Your daddy did it for you." But it wasn't an *accusation.*

_____

50. He *doused* them with syrup and began to eat. They tasted marvelous.

_____

Part II: Determining the Meaning   Match the vocabulary words to their dictionary definitions.

___ 41. conspiring   A. see; recognize
___ 42. sporadically   B. without stopping
___ 43. vanquished   C. drenched
___ 44. repented   D. took back; changed for the better
___ 45. discern   E. guilty charge
___ 46. relentlessly   F. terror
___ 47. dread   G. defeated
___ 48. dredging   H. plotting
___ 49. accusation   I. occasionally
___ 50. doused   J. bringing up; recalling

Vocabulary - *Bridge to Terabithia* Chapters 12-13

Part I: Using Prior Knowledge and Contextual Clues
Below are the sentences in which the vocabulary words appear in the text. Read the sentence. Use any clues you can find in the sentence combined with your prior knowledge, and write what you think the underlined words mean on the lines provided.

51. He went into the bedroom and felt under the mattress until he *retrieved* all his paper and paints that Leslie had given him at Christmastime.

_____

52. P.T. was left crying *piteously* in the other side.

_____

53. The coldness inside of him had moved upward into his throat *constricting* it.

_____

54. "Father, into Thy hands I *commend* her spirit." He knew Leslie would have liked those words.

_____

55. The same quiet, assuring voice of the *paramedics* on Emergency, but his heart was bongoing against his chest.

_____

56. Even after they'd given up trying to make Leslie miserable, they'd kept on *despising* her- as though there was one of them worth the nail on Leslie's toe.

_____

57. And even he himself had entertained the traitorous thought that now he would be the fastest.

_____

Bridge to Terabithia Vocabulary Chapters 12-13 Continued

58. He looked up into her face, *despite* himself.

_____

59. Mrs. Myers loving, *mourning*. How could you picture it?

_____

60. Handle with care-everything-even the *predators*.

_____

Part II: Determining the Meaning   Match the vocabulary words to their dictionary definitions.

___ 51. retrieved   A. tightening
___ 52. piteously   B. gathered; recovered
___ 53. constricting   C. entrust; commit
___ 54. commend   D. those who live off preying on others
___ 55. paramedics   E. pitifully
___ 56. despising   F. disloyal; back-stabbing
___ 57. traitorous   G. grieving
___ 58. despite   H. emergency medical persons
___ 59. mourning   I. in spite of
___ 60. predators   J. hating

ANSWER KEY - VOCABULARY
Bridge to Terabithia

Chapters 1, 2
1. C
2. G
3. D
4. E
5. I
6. F
7. H
8. J
9. B
10. A

Chapters 3, 4
11. E
12. I
13. F
14. D
15. H
16. G
17. J
18. A
19. C
20. B

Chapters 5, 6
21. C
22. G
23. F
24. H
25. I
26. E
27. B
28. A
29. J
30. D

Chapters 7, 8
31. H
32. D
33. A
34. F
35. G
36. E
37. B
38. J
39. I
40. C

Chapters 9-11
41. H
42. I
43. G
44. D
45. A
46. B
47. F
48. J
49. E
50. C

Chapters 12, 13
51. B
52. E
53. A
54. C
55. H
56. J
57. F
58. I
59. G
60. D

DAILY LESSONS

LESSON ONE

Objectives
1. To introduce the *Bridge to Terabithia* unit
2. To distribute books and other related materials
3. To introduce the theme of "people need friends"
4. To give students the opportunity to write to inform by developing and organizing facts to convey information

NOTE: Prior to Lesson One you need to have assigned students to bring to class pictures showing things that friends do for each other. Also, you should have an empty bulletin board with just background paper and the title: Bridge to Terabithia: A STORY ABOUT FRIENDSHIP.

Activity #1

Tell students to get out the pictures they were assigned to bring to class. Have each student post his picture(s) on the bulletin board and, as he does so, to explain to the class what trait of friendship his picture exemplifies.

TRANSITION: Explain to students that *Bridge to Terabithia*, the book they are about to read, is a story about friendship--about what it really means to be someone's friend and to have a friend.

Activity #2

Distribute Writing Assignment #1 and discuss the directions in detail. Give students the remainder of this class period to work on this assignment. While students are working on this assignment, distribute/assign the books to students. (If you wish, you may also distribute the other materials which students will need for the unit. There is, however, time planned for distributing materials in Lesson Two. If your students tend to lose materials or tend to forget to bring what they need to class, you might wait to give the materials out in Lesson Two when you will also need students' attention to tell them how these materials are to be used.)

WRITING ASSIGNMENT #1 - *Bridge to Terabithia*

PROMPT

Individuality can sometimes lead to loneliness. The two main characters in *Bridge to Terabithia* are both children who are a little different; they don't really "fit in." Their determination and imaginations create a bond; demonstrating what it means to be a friend and to have a friend. Friendship has great rewards, but being a friend isn't always easy.

Your assignment is to design an advertisement -- "WANTED: A FRIEND." Your advertisement should carry all the usual information in a "want ad": what you want, a job description, the requirements and the rewards. Your ad must fit on an 8 1/2" X 11" sheet of paper. Be as creative as you like, but remember your ad must contain the information requested above and remember that you are striving for an effective advertisement.

PREWRITING

The first thing you need to do is to jot down ideas you have about what a friend's job description would contain. What does it mean to be a friend? What qualities are necessary for a person to have to be a good friend? What are the positive aspects of being a friend? What are the difficult parts of the job?

Put down all of your thoughts, and then go back and sort through them. Combine ideas that are essentially the same. Organize your thoughts into categories: job description, qualifications/requirements, and rewards. From there you can begin to design your ad.

DRAFTING

You need to make a few basic decisions: Are you going to have any graphics (drawings) in your ad? What will be the attention-getter in your ad? How can you make all of your most important information fit on one page? How will you lay-out or design your ad? (How will it look on the page?) Once you have decided these things, you can put pencil to paper and make a rough draft of your ad.

PROMPT

After you have finished a rough draft of your ad, revise it yourself until you are happy with your work. Then, ask a student who sits near you to tell you what he/she likes best about your work, and what things he/she thinks can be improved. Take another look at your ad keeping in mind your critic's suggestions, and make the revisions you feel are necessary.

PROOFREADING

Do a final proofreading of your paper double-checking your grammar, spelling, organization, and the clarity of your ideas.

LESSON TWO

Objectives
1. To distribute and discuss the materials students will use in this unit
2. To do the prereading work for chapters 1 and 2
3. To model effective oral reading skills by reading chapter 1 aloud to the class
4. To have students identify the setting and point of view
5. To give students the opportunity to respond to chapter 1 by sharing similar family interactions

Activity #1

Distribute the materials students will use in this unit. Explain in detail how students are to use these materials.

Study Guides Students should preview the study guide questions before each reading assignment to get a feeling for what events and ideas are important in that section. After reading the section, students will (as a class or individually) answer the questions to review the important events and ideas from that section of the book. Students should keep the study guides as study materials for the unit test.

Vocabulary Prior to reading a reading assignment, students will do vocabulary work related to the section of the book they are about to read. Following the completion of the reading of the book, there will be a vocabulary review of all the words used in the vocabulary assignments. Students should keep their vocabulary work as study materials for the unit test.

Reading Assignment Sheet You need to fill in the reading assignment sheet to let students know when their reading has to be completed. You can either write the assignment sheet on a side blackboard or bulletin board and leave it there for students to see each day, or you can "ditto" copies for each student to have. In either case, you should advise students to become very familiar with the reading assignments so they know what is expected of them.

Extra Activities Center The Unit Resources of this unit contains suggestions for a library of related books and articles in your classroom as well as crossword and word search puzzles. Make an extra activities center in your room where you will keep these materials for students to use. (Bring the books and articles in from the library and keep several copies of the puzzles on hand.) Explain to students that these materials are available for students to use when they finish reading assignments or other class work early.

Nonfiction Assignment Sheet Explain to students that they each are to read at least one non-fiction piece from the in-class library at some time during the unit. Students will fill out a nonfiction assignment sheet after completing the reading to help you evaluate their reading experiences and to help the students think about and evaluate their own reading experiences.

Books Each school has its own rules and regulations regarding student use of school books. Advise students of the procedures that are normal for your school.

Activity #2

Have students complete the prereading work for chapters 1 and 2 of *Bridge to Terabithia* in pairs. They should review the study questions and do the required vocabulary work.

Activity #3

Read chapter 1 aloud to the class stopping to have them identify point of view and setting. When finished reading, give the class the opportunity to respond to the events and characters in this chapter by sharing similar personal family experiences.

Activity #4

Assign the reading of chapter 2 before the next class session.

LESSON THREE

Objectives
1. To review the main events and ideas from chapters 1 and 2
2. To preview the study questions for chapters 3 and 4
3. To familiarize students with the vocabulary in chapters 3 and 4
4. To begin the reading of chapter 3

Activity #1

Discuss the answers to the study questions for chapters 1 and 2 in detail. Write the answers on the board or overhead transparency so students can have the correct answers for study purposes.
Note: It is a good practice in public speaking and leadership skills for individual students to take charge of leading the discussions of the study questions. Perhaps a different student could go to the front of the class and lead the discussion each day that the study questions are discussed during this unit. Of course, the teacher should guide the discussion when appropriate and be sure to fill in any gaps the students leave.

Activity #2

Give students the remaining class time to preview the study questions for chapters 3 and 4 of *Bridge to Terabithia* and to do the related vocabulary work. If time allows, begin reading chapter 3 or assign the reading of chapters 3 and 4 to be completed prior to the next class session.

LESSON FOUR

Objectives
1. To review the main events and ideas from chapters 3 and 4
2. To familiarize students with vocabulary from chapters 5 and 6
3. To preview study questions for chapters 5 and 6

Activity #1

Use the multiple choice format of the study guide questions for chapters 3 and 4 as a quiz to check that students have done the required reading and to review the main ideas of chapters 3 and 4. Exchange papers for checking. Discuss answers and make sure students take notes for studying purposes.

Activity #2

Have students look over the prereading vocabulary work for chapters 5 and 6 for about 10 minutes. Use the matching section of the vocabulary pages as a springboard for a game similar to concentration. Divide students into groups of four or five. Have students quickly copy the vocabulary words (divide the task into sections to expedite) and their clues on separate index cards. Turn them all over. Have students in their small groups take turns flipping over two of the cards. If they are a match, i.e. a vocabulary word matches with its meaning, they keep the pair and get another turn. Students may look at the vocabulary words in their sentences for contextual clues. Continue play until all cards are matched into sets.

Activity #3

Give students any remaining time to look over study questions for chapters 5 and 6. Be sure they have read these chapters by Lesson Six class time.

LESSON FIVE

Objectives
1. To give students the opportunity to practice writing to express personal ideas
2. To draw attention to the theme of personal growth through creativity and imagination
3. To give students the opportunity to fulfill their nonfiction reading assignment

Activity #1

Distribute Writing Assignment #2 and discuss the directions in detail. Allow remaining class time for students to work on the assignment. Inform them this paper will be due by Lesson Seven so you will have time to evaluate them before their writing conference to be held during Lesson Ten. Students who finish early but have not completed their nonfiction reading form could go to the library at this time to find an appropriate selection.

NONFICTION READING ASSIGNMENT SHEET - *Bridge to Terabithia*
(To be completed after reading the required nonfiction article)

Name _____ Date _____

Title of Nonfiction Read _____

Written By _____ Publication Date _____

I. Factual Summary: Write a short summary of the piece you read.

II. Vocabulary
   1. With which vocabulary words in the piece did you encounter some degree of difficulty?

   2. How did you resolve your lack of understanding with these words?

III. Interpretation: What was the main point the author wanted you to get from reading his work?

IV. Criticism
   1. With which points of the piece did you agree or find easy to accept? Why?

   2. With which points of the piece did you disagree or find difficult to believe? Why?

V. Personal Response: What do you think about this piece? OR How does this piece influence your ideas?

WRITING ASSIGNMENT #2 - *Bridge To Terabithia*

PROMPT

We all long for a special place of our own or to share with those we care for: a tropical paradise, a wilderness escape, or an apartment in Manhattan. Everyone's choice is different and reflects their personal tastes and values. Jesse and Leslie invent a secret make-believe kingdom where they reign supreme. They even make Leslie's puppy the guardian of their kingdom.

Your assignment is to describe your ideal getaway, the place you would like to be able to retreat to whenever you could; alone or with someone you enjoy and trust. Let your creativity flow; do not limit the possibilities. Remember fantasies are only limited by the extent of your imagination.

PREWRITING

A good way to start is to think about what type of place attracts you. Would you like to be royalty in a castle and kingdom like Leslie and Jesse or would you rather be a hermit on an isolated island? What would you like to have happen in your fantasy place more than anything else? Jot down what that is on a piece of paper. Make notes about the details of your ideal place and your role there.

DRAFTING

You should begin your paper with an introductory paragraph giving your reader some information describing your dream place. Use your notes about the details of your fantasy to help you get started. Include why you would choose this specific place.

The body of your composition should contain descriptive information about the details of your special place: the location, the climate, the mood, any structure you might want, who you would like to share it with, and your role there, etc.

Write a final paragraph in which you conclude how this special place would make you feel. Why and how it would be important to you? How would visiting this place make you happy, inspired, content, excited, etc.?

PROMPT

When you finish the rough draft of your paper, ask a student who sits near you to read it. After reading your rough draft, he/she should tell you what he/she liked best about your work, which parts were difficult to understand, and ways in which your work could be improved. Reread your paper considering your critic's comments, and make the corrections you think are necessary.

PROOFREADING

Do a final proofreading of your paper double-checking your grammar, spelling, organization, and the clarity of your ideas.

LESSON SIX

Objectives
1. To review the main ideas of chapters 5 and 6
2. To do the prereading vocabulary work and study questions for chapters 7 and 8
3. To expose students to figurative language

Activity #1

Hand out four little slips of paper or mini cards to each student that have the letters A, B, C, or D on them. A good idea is to use different color cards for each letter. Use the multiple choice study guide questions and answers on Chapters 5 and 6 for an oral review. Read the question (and/ or show it on the overhead). Then give students the four possible answers, labeling them A, B, C, or D (or show on overhead again). Students respond by holding up the card with what they think is the correct answer. This is one variety of Every Student Response. Remind students not to look at what others are holding up, but to simply display the card of their choice. This is a quick indicator of students' comprehension. You can make it somewhat different by requiring complete silence and having them read the questions silently from the overhead, or make it more mysterious (fun?) by blindfolding everyone and have them hold up a certain number of fingers per answer instead of using the cards.

Activity #2

Have students pair up and do the prereading work together for chapters 7 and 8.

Activity #3

Give students remaining time to review chapters 7 and 8 study guide questions. Inform them that the completion of the reading of these chapters is due by class Lesson Eight.

Activity #4

Within the last 5-8 minutes of class, turn the class's attention to your reading of the following examples of figurative language from their recent reading (just ask them to listen):
- *he acted like the original yellow-bellied sapsucker*
- *it would be like putting a veil on the Mona Lisa*
- *the Millsburg First National was sitting around begging him to crack it*
- *smiled like a plastic angel*
- *her anger came rocketing to the surface*
- *being Mrs. Myers' pet was pure poison*
- *surprise swooshed up from the class like steam from a released radiator cap*

Inquire if they see any similarities in these passages, or have any idea what these are examples of? Encourage them to do some research tonight if no one comes up with "figures of speech" (personification, etc.) or "figurative language". Tell them that in the next class session they will become very familiar with these and many more passages like them from their novel.

LESSON SEVEN

Objectives
1. To introduce simile, personification, and metaphor as figures of speech
2. To distinguish between three different types of figurative language
3. To have students locate figurative language in the text
4. To create original figures of speech
5. To illustrate figurative language

Activity #1

Review any of the previous introduction that was successful. If any students identified the passages correctly, continue allowing them to explain. If not, once again read some examples from the text and determine what makes them figurative language. Make three columns on the chalkboard labeling each one separately: simile, metaphor, and personification. Spend some time here instructing about these three forms of figurative language. Perhaps you could cite some examples from familiar songs. Ask why they think any author or lyricist would use them? Do they use them? Why? In what way does using them enhance speaking or writing or the understanding of each of these. As a whole group, have students give you examples they can think of and then have them locate a few in any part of the text they have read. Allow them to come to the board and write these under the correct heading. When you are satisfied with their ability to recognize them go to the next activity.

Activity #2

Divide the class into small groups of three or four. Have each group assign a recorder. Give them a couple of sheets of paper. Ask each group to locate as many of these figures of speech as they can from the text. They may be more successful in the portion they already have read, but it isn't necessary to limit them. Giving them a time constraint is an option. It could be a race, you are the judge. Offer a special incentive for the group that can most quickly find the figurative language-rich beginning chapter page that has two similes, three personifications, and one metaphor. You may want to rule out using the ones that are posted on the board. It's up to you. There are a wealth of them present in the text, they'll find plenty. Wrap this activity up by having the group with the **most** read their list aloud. Decide as a whole group if indeed each one is correct. Have all groups check off the ones that are read that they also found. Allow every group to read any that have not yet been mentioned. You could give small treats for first, second, third place, etc.

Activity #3

Have students create one example of each type. They could be individual sentences or you could require them to write a short paragraph using all three. Base this on the ability level of your students and/or time. Create one together as a model. If time, have them illustrate it with original art work or magazine pictures. Save finished products for display. They could do this part as homework.

FIGURATIVE LANGUAGE TEST - *Bridge to Terabithia*

I. Read the following examples of figurative language. Label each one separately with either an **S** for simile, **P** for personification, or an **M** for metaphor. **BONUS**: Circle the **5** that are both an S and a P. *Super Sleuth Award*: Locate **one** that contains more than one of all three types.

1. Jess scooped up the sodden dog and shoved him rear-first into the cave of Leslie's raincoat. _____
2. He wondered what it would be like to have a mother whose stories were inside her head instead of marching across the television screen all day long._____
3. Dread lay on Jesse's stomach like a hunk of cold, undigested doughnut._____
4. May Belle was as scrawny as Brenda was fat._____
5. Her eyes were still drooped from sleep, and her pale brown hair stuck up all over her head like a squirrel's nest on a winter branch. _____
6. I'll just grab that old terror by the shoulders and shake the daylights out of it. _____
7. Entering the gallery was like stepping into the pine grove._____
8. I was beginning to think the sun had gone into a cave and vowed never to return, like the Japanese myth._____
9. The western sun danced on the windshield dazzling his eyes._____
10. The words exploded in his head like corn against the sides of the popper._____
11. Jess gave himself over to the numbness that was buzzing to be let out from a corner of his brain._____
12. Leslie would come to open it P. T. jumping at her heels like a star around the moon._____
13. The coldness curled up inside of him and flopped over. _____
14. May Belle sat down again as though slapped down by her mother's voice._____
15. The paints floated on top, riding the current like a boat, but the papers swirled about, soaking in the muddy water, being sucked down, around, and down. _____
16. Like in *The Ten Commandments* on TV when the water came rushing into the dry path Moses made and swept all the Egyptians away, the long dry bed of the creek was a roaring eight-foot-wide sea, sweeping before it great branches of trees, logs, and trash, swirling them about like so many Egyptian chariots, the hungry waters licking and sometimes leaping the banks, daring them to try to confine it. _____
17. Brenda and Ellie looked like a pair of peacocks with fake tail feathers._____
18. Like a single bird across a stormcloud sky, a tiny peace winged its way through the chaos inside his body._____
19. But as a regular thing, as a permanent place, this was where he would choose to be- here where the dogwood and redbud played hide and seek between the oaks and evergreens, and the sun flung itself in golden streams through the tree to splash warmly at their feet._____
20. Jess leaned back and drank in the rich, clear color of the sky._____
21. Just walking down the hill toward the woods made something warm and liquid steal through his body. _____
22. Lord, May Belle, I was shaking like Jello._____
23. Her Leslie smile shifted suddenly and ominously into a scowl that silenced the storm._____
24. Gary lowered his head like a bull._____
25. It was as though he had swallowed grasshoppers._____

II. List one example of your own for each type of figurative language. They can be original or from your favorite songs.

ANSWER KEY- FIGURATIVE LANGUAGE TEST - *Bridge to Terabithia*

I.
1. M
2. P
3. P, S
4. S
5. S
6. P
7. S
8. P, S
9. P
10. P, S
11. P
12. S
13. P
14. S
15. P, S
16. S, P, M, P, S, P
17. S
18. S, P
19. P
20. P
21. P
22. S
23. P
24. S
25. S

II. Answers will vary.

LESSON EIGHT

Objectives
1. To review main events and ideas in chapters 7 and 8
2. To do the prereading vocabulary work for chapters 9-11
3. To preview study guide questions for chapters 9-11
4. To give students practice in making predictions

Activity #1

Use the multiple choice study guide questions as a quiz to test students reading of assigned text and as a review of the main ideas. Exchange papers to check. Discuss answers to insure understanding. Encourage note taking for their later study use.

Activity #2

Have students spend about 10 minutes completing the prereading vocabulary page. After they have done that, pair them up. Have one member of each pair "act" out one of the words, while the other one tries to guess the word. Do this until all of the vocabulary words have been covered at least once. This is similar to the game Charades. If extra time, include vocabulary from earlier chapters.

Activity #3

Hand out slips of paper to each student. Have them predict upcoming events in chapters 9-11. Collect the predictions and keep until after you have read the following chapters and discussed.

Activity #4

Have students preview study guide questions independently for chapters 9-11 in the remaining class time.

LESSON NINE

Objectives
1. To read chapters 9-11
2. To give students practice reading orally
3. To evaluate students' oral reading

Activity #1

Have students read chapters 9-11 orally in class. (It is likely you won't finish all three chapters, Lesson 9 builds in time for the students to finish the reading.) You probably know the best way to get readers within your class; pick students at random, ask for volunteers, have students who have just read select another student, assign numbers to students and spin a spinner, whatever works best for you. Complete the oral reading evaluation form that follows this lesson after listening to your students read.

ORAL READING EVALUATION - *Bridge to Terabithia*

Name _____ Class____ Date _____

SKILL	EXCELLENT	GOOD	AVERAGE	FAIR	POOR
Fluency	5	4	3	2	1
Clarity	5	4	3	2	1
Audibility	5	4	3	2	1
Pronunciation	5	4	3	2	1
_____	5	4	3	2	1
_____	5	4	3	2	1

Total _____ Grade _____

Comments:

LESSON TEN

Objectives
1. To evaluate students' writing
2. To give students an opportunity to produce an error-free paper and to apply the teacher's suggestions
3. To complete the reading of chapters 9-11

Activity #1

Allow students to finish reading the chapters started yesterday silently at their desks. If they finish this, have them put the finishing touches on their Writing Assignment #1 Want Ads. They will be sharing these in Lesson 13.

Activity #2

Call students to your desk (or some other private area) to discuss their papers from Writing Assignment 2. Use the following Writing Evaluation Form to help structure your conference.

Activity #3

After the writing conference, allow students to revise their papers using your suggestions and corrections. Give them about three days from the date they receive their papers to complete the revision. I suggest grading the revisions on an A-C-E scale (all revisions well-done, some revisions made, few or no revisions made). This will speed your grading time and still give some credit for the students' efforts. Give students a date for when revisions are due.

WRITING EVALUATION FORM - *Bridge to Terabithia*

Name _____ Date _____

Writing Assignment #1 for the *Bridge to Terabithia* unit   Grade _____

Circle One For Each Item:

Description (paragraph 1)	excellent	good	fair	poor
Plans (body paragraphs)	excellent	workable	fair	not realistic
Conclusion	excellent	good	fair	poor
Grammar:	excellent	good	fair	poor (errors noted)
Spelling:	excellent	good	fair	poor (errors noted)
Punctuation:	excellent	good	fair	poor (errors noted)
Legibility:	excellent	good	fair	poor

Strengths:

Weaknesses:

Comments/Suggestions:

LESSON ELEVEN

Objectives
1. To preview the study guide questions for chapters 12 and 13
2. To preview the prereading vocabulary work for chapters 12 and 13
3. To discuss grief and its stages
4. To assign reading of chapters 12 and 13

Activity #1

Have students spend approximately 10 minutes completing the prereading vocabulary work independently. Pass out plain paper for drawing, or use individual easels or slates. Have one of the partners sketch their impression of one of the vocabulary words within a limited amount of time. The other one is to guess which vocabulary word he/she is trying to picture. When the correct word has been chosen, play turns to the other partner. Continue play until all vocabulary has been covered for chapters 12 and 13. This is similar to the game Pictionary. It could also be done in small groups. Once again, if time, incorporate vocabulary from earlier chapters.

Activity #2

Individually, have students look over the study guide questions for chapters 12 and 13. From these questions, they will be able to tell that these chapters are about Jesse coming to terms with Leslie's death.

Activity #3

Point out that it is not easy accepting the death of someone you care a great deal about. Even though dying is a part of the process of living, it is a difficult time for those left behind. It is normal to experience many different feelings during this time. Explain that through reading chapters 12 and 13 they will become aware of the various stages someone may go through dealing with the death of a loved one, as they read about Jesse's feelings, thoughts, and actions.

At this time, if you are comfortable with it, you might share a personal experience or allow a willing student to share an experience. The goal is not to turn class into a teary mass, but to expose the students to the emotional side of grieving and its purpose. Perhaps the various stages of grief, and you or your student's experience with them, could be graphically represented on a chart or blackboard. Ask students, as they read chapters 12 and 13, to jot down the feelings, thoughts, and actions of Jesse as he comes to grips with Leslie's drowning (disbelief, denial, blame, anger, guilt, acceptance, etc.).

Activity #4

Assign reading of chapters 12 and 13 before the next class session.

LESSON TWELVE

Objectives
1. To review the main ideas and events from chapters 12 and 13
2. To chart Jesse's grieving (feelings, thoughts, and actions) from these chapters

Activity #1

Have students pair up and quiz each other's comprehension using the study guide questions or the multiple choice format.

Activity #2

Have the class retrieve their notes from the recent reading concerning Jesse's reactions to Leslie's death. Divide the class into 9 small groups and have each group list responses for a different topic. Ideas for topics could be: Jesse's immediate feelings when told-his immediate actions-his immediate thoughts. Jesse's feelings-thoughts-and actions when he and his family went to the Burke's house and right afterwards. Finally his feelings-thoughts and actions when he goes back to Terabithia. This would be enough for 9 groups. If you have less groups, assign each group more than one topic.

Activity #3

Ask a representative to share the findings of each group while you or a student chart his reactions on the board or chart paper. Compare his responses to the ones shared and discussed yesterday. Obvious similarities will be present.

TIME	FEELINGS	THOUGHTS	ACTIONS
Immediately after being told			
At the Burke's and right afterwards			
Upon returning to Terabithia			

LESSON THIRTEEN

Objectives
1. To give students the opportunity to share and display their Want Ads
2. To give students the opportunity to write to persuade

Activity #1
    Ask students individually, or in pairs (if they are more comfortable) to stand and share their Want Ads for a friend. Post in a designated area. If the climate of friendly competition is right, vote on a few or one winning poster. Have the class decide on the criteria and the reward.

Activity #2
    Distribute Writing Assignment #3 and discuss the directions in detail. Give students the remainder of class time to work on this assignment. Provide them with a due date.

WRITING ASSIGNMENT #3 - *Bridge to Terabithia*

PROMPT

    Jesse Aarons was a frustrated artist. His father disapproved of his drawing, and he did not get any support from the rest of his family. The only two people who encouraged him were Leslie and his music teacher, Miss Edmunds. Through the course of the novel, it appeared that he and his father were able to grow closer through the tragedy of Leslie's death.

    In this writing assignment, pretend you are Jesse Aarons, Jr., and Miss Edmunds has offered you the opportunity of attending a special art school during the upcoming summer. There is no charge to your family and she will handle the transportation. It is your objective to convince your parents to allow you to attend. You are thrilled with the possibility of being able to pursue your dream.

PREWRITING

    To begin with, list all the reasons why you feel you should be able to attend this special art school. Decide which are your strongest justifiable arguments, and which are less substantial. Organize your points from weaker to strongest and jot down anything you can think of which will support or explain your arguments.

DRAFTING

    Begin with an introductory paragraph in which you express your strong desire to be able to attend the summer art school. Follow that with one paragraph for each of the main points you have to support your side of this argument. Fill in each paragraph with examples, facts, and feelings that support your main point. Then, write an ending paragraph in which you summarize your arguments and restate your intense longing and need to take advantage of Miss Edmunds' offer.

PROMPT

    When you finish the rough draft of your paper, ask a student who sits near you to read it. After reading your rough draft, he\she should tell you what he\she liked best about your work, which parts were difficult to understand, and ways in which your work could be improved. Reread your paper considering your critic's comments, and make the corrections you think are necessary.

PROOFREADING

    Do a final proofreading of your paper double-checking your grammar, spelling, organization, and the clarity of your ideas.

LESSONS FOURTEEN AND FIFTEEN

Objectives
1. To discuss the ideas and themes from *Bridge to Terabithia* in greater detail
2. To have students exercise their interpretive and critical thinking skills
3. To try to relate some of the ideas in *Bridge to Terabithia* to the students' lives

Activity #1

Choose the questions from the Extra Discussion Questions/Writing Assignments which seem most appropriate for your students. A class discussion of these questions is most effective if students have been given the opportunity to formulate answers to the questions prior to the discussion. To this end, you may either have all the students formulate answers to all the questions, divide your class into groups and assign one or more questions to each group, or you could assign one question to each student in your class. The option you choose will make a difference in the amount of class time needed for this activity.

Activity #2

After students have had ample time to formulate answers to the questions, begin your class discussion of the questions and the ideas presented by the questions. Be sure students take notes during the discussion so they have information to study for the unit test.

EXTRA DISCUSSION QUESTIONS/WRITING ASSIGNMENTS - *Bridge to Terabithia*

Interpretive

1. From what point of view is this story told? How would the story change if told from only one character's point of view?

2. Identify the setting. How does it influence the plot of this novel?

3. Are the characters in *Bridge to Terabithia* stereotypes? If so, explain why an author would include stereotypes in a book. If they are not, explain how they merit individuality.

4. What are the main conflicts in the story, and how are they resolved?

5. What is foreshadowing? Give examples of foreshadowing used in *Bridge to Terabithia*.

6. Why do you think the dog was introduced to the storyline?

7. Complete a character sketch for both Jesse and Leslie.

8. Formulate an accurate timeline for the novel beginning with the August/September fifth grade started for Jesse and Leslie.

9. Explain the role of each of these characters: May Belle, Janice Avery, Mr. and Mrs. Burke, Mr. and Mrs. Aarons, Miss Edmunds, and Mrs. Myers.

10. Define climax. Next, summarize the main events leading up to **it** and the remaining events after **it** that create the resolution.

11. Locate examples of the northern Virginia dialect the characters use. Did its use influence your opinion of the characters?

Critical

12. Explain the significance of the title "*Bridge to Terabithia*".

13. Even though there was no job to go to, Jesse's dad left every morning early to look. What does this say about Mr. Aarons?

14. Compare and contrast the characters' lifestyle in northern Virginia in the 1970's to your lifestyle today.

15. Why do you think Jesse decided to befriend Leslie after avoiding her initially?

Bridge to Terabithia Extra Discussion Questions page 2

16. Compare and contrast Leslie and Jesse's family makeup, beliefs, and values.

17. "This one perfect day of his life was worth anything he had to pay." These were Jesse's thoughts on the way to Washington with Miss Edmunds. Why did the author include them?

18. For what reason do you think Katherine Paterson includes some bad words in this book for young readers?

19. There are some religious issues and Biblical references in this novel. After reading a short biography of Katherine Paterson, tell why she is comfortable writing about these things.

20. Who is responsible for Leslie's death? Defend your answer.

21. Describe Katherine Paterson's writing style, including her use of figurative language. How does it shape the story?

22. Is the story of *Bridge to Terabithia* believable? Why or why not?

23. Discover what motivated Katherine Paterson to write a book about the death of a child.

24. What was symbolic about the Indian/buffalo display at the Smithsonian that attracted Jesse?

25. What universal themes appear in *Bridge to Terabithia*?

26. Explain why the author included this statement of Leslie's after Easter Sunday church, "It's crazy, isn't it? You have to believe it, but you hate it. I don't have to believe it, and I think it's beautiful. It's crazy."

Critical/ Personal Response

27. Why did Jesse's dad disapprove of him wanting to become an artist? Would a father think differently today? Why or why not? How would your parents feel if you wanted to be an artist? Would you enjoy this sort of work? Explain.

28. Will Jesse "pay back to the world in beauty and caring what Leslie loaned him in vision and strength" like he says on page 126? Support your answer.

29. Have you read any other books written by Katherine Paterson? How do they compare to *Bridge to Terabithia*? Which one is your favorite? Why?

Bridge to Terabithia Extra Discussion Questions page 3

30. Were you surprised at Jesse's reaction to Leslie's tale of woe about Janice Avery? Who did you expect to have more sympathy in that type of situation? What does this tell us about Jesse's character?

31. Janice Avery broke the rule that you never mixed up troubles at home with life at school. Do you think this has changed since the Seventies? Why or why not?

Personal Response

32. Jesse experiences a number of different feelings dealing with Leslie's death. Do you think this is abnormal? Have you ever been through a similar experience? Please share.

33. Have you ever had some sort of recognition like Jesse's fourth grade April 22nd race victory? If so, were you motivated to continue to be recognized, like Jesse who got up early every day in the summer to practice running?

34. What is the value of believing in yourself and developing your own special talents, despite the criticisms and misunderstanding of those around you?

35. When Jesse returns from Washington and gets the news about Leslie he wishes he would have invited her to come along with him and Miss Edmunds. Have you ever regretted not doing something?

36. Jesse felt Leslie was his other, more exciting self- his way to Terabithia and all the worlds beyond. Have you ever had a friend like that?

37. If you were Jesse, how would you handle May Belle's adoration?

38. Do you or someone you know have four or more siblings of the opposite sex? What is it like to be the only boy or girl in a family dominated by the other?

39. How would you have handled the problems with Janice Avery?

40. Jesse becomes very upset with himself because he feels he is "gutless." Are you hard on yourself about some weakness you think you have?

41. Did you ever dress up a younger sibling and wheel them around in a baby carriage like Ellie and Brenda did to Jesse when he was little?

Bridge to Terabithia Extra Discussion Questions page 4

Quotations

1. "All right, Jesse. Get your lazy self off that bench. Miss Bessie's bag is probably dragging ground by now. And you got beans to pick."

2. "What are they teaching you in that damn school? Bunch of old ladies turning my only son into some kind of a-"

3. "You're the proverbial diamond in the rough."

4. "Ellie bought herself a see-through blouse, and Momma's throwing a fit!"

5. "Sometimes like the Barbie doll you need to give people something that's for them, not just something that makes you feel good giving it."

6. " It was up to him to pay back the world in beauty and caring what Leslie had loaned him in vision and strength."

7. "Whatsa matter Fulcher? Scared to see her run?"

8. "My parents are reassessing their value structure."

9. "I am sure that all of you were as impressed as I was with Leslie's exciting essay."

10. "Don't look like there'll be room across the back here for you and Janice Avery."

11. "We need a place so secret that we would never tell anyone in the whole world about it."

12. "You might want to tell Joyce Ann sometime."

13. "It's the principle of the thing, Jess. That's what you've got to understand. You have to stop people like that. Otherwise they turn into tyrants and dictators."

14. "This is not an ordinary place. Even the rulers of Terabithia come into it only at times of greatest sorrow or of greatest joy. We must strive to keep it sacred"

15. "Then we'll name him Prince Terrien and make him the guardian of Terabithia."

16. "It's really great. Really. I just ain't got the hang of it yet."

Bridge to Terabithia Extra Discussion Questions page 5

17. "Cheap junk. don't get nothing for your money these days."

18. "I don't know what I'd do without Ellie. She's the only one of you ever cares whether I live or die."

19. "If she was an animal predator, we'd we obliged to help her."

20. "I'd be obliged if you'd finish milking and come on back to the house."

21. "It felt like Christmas again."

22. "It's crazy, isn't it? You have to believe it, but you hate it. I don't have to believe it, and I think it's beautiful. It's crazy."

23. "But Leslie, what if you die? What's going to happen to you if you die?.

24. "Dost know what is in my mind, O king? Methinks some evil being has put a curse on our beloved kingdom."

25. "Who's afraid of the big bad wolf? Tra-la-la-la-la."

26. "Hey maybe you could go down to the medical college and get a gut transplant."

27. "Great, my life has been worthwhile after all."

28. "What little girl?"

29. "She had tricked him. She had made him leave is old self behind and come into her world, and then before he was really at home in it but too late to go back, she had left him stranded there- like an astronaut wandering about on the moon. Alone."

30. "I am now the fastest runner in the fifth grade."

31. "It ain't the same for dogs. It's like the smarter you are, the more things can scare you."

32. "Hell, ain't it? Lord, boy, don't be a fool. God ain't gonna send any little girls to hell."

33. "Leslie, I'm just a dumb dodo, and you know it! What am I supposed to do?"

Bridge to Terabithia Extra Discussion Questions page 6

34. "Father, into Thy hands I commend her spirit."

35. This morning when I came in, someone had already taken out her desk. It-it-we- I never had such a student. In all my years of teaching. I shall always be grateful."

36. "It was Leslie who had taken him from the cow pasture into Terabithia and turned him into a king. He had thought that was it. Wasn't king the best you could be? Now it occurred to him that perhaps Terabithia was like a castle when you came to be knighted. After you stayed for a while and grew strong you had to move on. For hadn't Leslie, even in Terabithia, tried to push back the walls of his mind and make him see beyond to the shining world-huge and terrible and beautiful and very fragile?

LESSON SIXTEEN

<u>Objective</u>
1. To complete discussions begun in Lessons Fourteen and Fifteen
2. To allow students time to complete extra activities of their choice
3. To give students the opportunity to share Writing Assignments #2 or #3

<u>Activity #1</u>
Since Lesson Fourteen and part of Lesson Fifteen were taken up with giving students time to formulate answers, you will need this class period to complete your class discussions.

<u>Activity #2</u>
Allow students to select an activity of their choice from the Extra Activities. Also encourage students to create an activity of their own that corresponds to this unit.

<u>Activity #3</u>
Give students who would like to share Writing Assignment #2 or# 3 the opportunity to read these orally.

LESSON SEVENTEEN

<u>Objectives</u>
To review all of the vocabulary work done in this unit

<u>Activity</u>
Choose one (or more) of the vocabulary review activities listed on the next page(s) and spend your class period as directed in the activity. Some of the materials for these review activities are located in the Vocabulary Resources section in this unit.

VOCABULARY REVIEW ACTIVITIES

1. Divide your class into two teams and have an old-fashioned spelling or definition bee.

2. Give each of your students (or students in groups of two, three or four) a *Bridge to Terabithia* Vocabulary Word Search Puzzle. The person (group) to find all of the vocabulary words in the puzzle first wins.

3. Give students a *Bridge to Terabithia* Vocabulary Word Search Puzzle without the word list. The person or group to find the most vocabulary words in the puzzle wins.

4. Use a *Bridge to Terabithia* Vocabulary Crossword Puzzle. Put the puzzle onto a transparency on the overhead projector (so everyone can see it), and do the puzzle together as a class.

5. Give students a *Bridge to Terabithia* Vocabulary Matching Work sheet to do.

6. Divide your class into two teams. Use the *Bridge to Terabithia* vocabulary words with their letters jumbled as a word list. Student 1 from Team A faces off against Student 1 from Team B. You write the first jumbled word on the board. The first student (1A or 1B) to unscramble the word wins the chance for his/her team to score points. If 1A wins the jumble, go to student 2A and give him/her a definition. He/she must give you the correct spelling of the vocabulary word which fits that definition. If he/she does, Team A scores a point, and you give student 3A a definition for which you expect a correctly spelled matching vocabulary word. Continue giving Team A definitions until some team member makes an incorrect response. An incorrect response sends the game back to the jumbled-word face off, this time with students 2A and 2B. Instead of repeating giving definitions to the first few students of each team, continue with the student after the one who gave the last incorrect response on the team. For example, if Team B wins the jumbled-word face-off, and student 5B gave the last incorrect answer for Team B, you would start this round of definition questions with student 6B, and so on. The team with the most points wins!

7. Have students write a story in which they correctly use as many vocabulary words as possible. Have students read their compositions orally. Post the most original compositions on your bulletin board.

LESSON EIGHTEEN

Objective
> To review the main ideas presented in *Bridge to Terabithia*

Activity #1
> Choose one of the review games/activities included in this unit and spend your class period as outlined there. Some materials for these activities are located in the Unit Resources section of this unit.

Activity #2
> Remind students that the Unit Test will be in the next class meeting. Stress the review of the Study Guides and their class notes as a last minute, brush-up review for the unit test.

REVIEW GAMES/ACTIVITIES - *Bridge to Terabithia*

1. Ask the class to make up a unit test for *Bridge to Terabithia*. The test should have 4 sections: matching, true/false, short answer, and essay. Students may use 1/2 period to make the test and then swap papers and use the other 1/2 class period to take a test a classmate has devised (open book). You may want to use the unit test included in this unit or take questions from the students' unit tests to formulate your own test.

2. Take 1/2 period for students to make up true and false questions (including the answers). Collect the papers and divide the class into two teams. Draw a big tic-tac-toe board on the chalk board. Make one team X and one team O. Ask questions to each side, giving each student one turn. If the question is answered correctly, that students' team's letter (X or O) is placed in the box. If the answer is incorrect, no mark is placed in the box. The object is to get three marks in a row like tic-tac-toe. You may want to keep track of the number of games won for each team.

3. Take 1/2 period for students to make up questions (true/false and short answer). Collect the questions. Divide the class into two teams. You'll alternate asking questions to individual members of teams A & B (like in a spelling bee). The question keeps going from A to B until it is correctly answered, then a new question is asked. A correct answer does not allow the team to get another question. Correct answers are +2 points; incorrect answers are -1 point.

4. Have students pair up and quiz each other from their study guides and class notes.

5. Give students a *Bridge to Terabithia* crossword puzzle to complete.

6. Divide your class into two teams. Use the *Bridge to Terabithia* crossword words with their letters jumbled as a word list. Student 1 from Team A faces off against Student 1 from Team B. You write the first jumbled word on the board. The first student (1A or 1B) to unscramble the word wins the chance for his/her team to score points. If 1A wins the jumble, go to student 2A and give him/her a clue. He/she must give you the correct word which matches that clue. If he/she does, Team A scores a point, and you give student 3A a clue for which you expect another correct response. Continue giving Team A clues until some team member makes an incorrect response. An incorrect response sends the game back to the jumbled-word face off, this time with students 2A and 2B. Instead of repeating giving clues to the first few students of each team, continue with the student after the one who gave the last incorrect response on the team. For example, if Team B wins the jumbled-word face-off, and student 5B gave the last incorrect answer for Team B, you would start this round of clue questions with student 6B, and so on.

LESSON NINETEEN

Objective
   To test the students' understanding of the main ideas and themes in *Bridge to Terabithia*

Activity #1
   Distribute the unit tests. Go over the instructions in detail and allow the students the entire class period to complete the exam.

Activity #2
   Collect all test papers and assigned books prior to the end of the class period.

NOTES ABOUT THE UNIT TESTS IN THIS UNIT:

   There are 5 different unit tests which follow.
   There are two short answer tests which are based primarily on facts from the novel. The answer key short for answer unit test 1 follows the student test. The answer key for short answer test 2 follows the student short answer unit test 2.
   There is one advanced short answer unit test. It is based on the extra discussion questions and quotations. Use the matching key for short answer unit test 2 to check the matching section of the advanced short answer unit test. There is no key for the short answer questions and quotations. The answers will be based on the discussions you have had during class.
   There are two multiple choice unit tests. Following the two unit tests, you will find an answer sheet on which students should mark their answers. The same answer sheet should be used for both tests; however, students' answers will be different for each test. Following the students' answer sheet for the multiple choice tests you will find your answer key.
   The short answer tests have a vocabulary section. You should choose 10 of the vocabulary words from this unit, read them orally and have the students write them down. Then, either have students write a definition or use the words in sentences.

   Use these words for the vocabulary section of the advanced short answer test:
nauseatingly	sporadically	consolidated
pandemonium	deliberately	proverbial
insufficiencies	relentlessly	constricting
hypocritical	traitorous	retrieved

UNIT TESTS

SHORT ANSWER UNIT TEST #1 - *Bridge to Terabithia*

I. Matching/Identify

___ 1. Paint Set   A. Leslie reigned as this over Terabithia

___ 2. Queen   B. Worships Jesse

___ 3. May Belle   C. Local elementary school

___ 4. Lumber   D. Entry into secret kingdom

___ 5. Lark Creek   E. Author

___ 6. Janice Avery   F. Christmas gift from Leslie to Jesse

___ 7. Guts   G. Jesse thinks he has none

___ 8. Drowned   H. Used to build a bridge over creek bed

___ 9. Paterson   I. Guardian of Terabithia

___ 10. Easter   J. When Leslie went to church with Jesse

___ 11. Rope Swing   K. Seventh grade bully

___ 12. Value Structure   L. Topic of Leslie's essay

___ 13. TV   M. How Leslie died

___ 14. Scuba Diving   N. Leslie's parents were reassessing these

___ 15. Prince Terrien   O. Burke's have none

II. Short Answer

1. Who is Miss Julia Edmunds and why is she special to Jesse?

Bridge to Terabithia Short Answer Unit Test 1 Page 2

2. What kind of relationship do Jesse and his father have?

3. What surprise occurs at recess on Leslie's first day at Lark Creek?

4. Why does the class give Leslie a hard time after Mrs. Myers assigns the TV program for homework?

5. How do Jesse's parents feel about his relationship with Leslie?

6. Why does Jesse become angry when Brenda criticizes Leslie?

7. In what way do Leslie and Jesse feel differently about their parents?

8. Jess and Leslie go to the pine grove after returning to their kingdom after a month's absence. Why?

9. What Lark Creek Elementary rule had Janice broken?

Bridge to Terabithia Short Answer Unit Test 1 page 3

10. On Wednesday why did Leslie think some evil being had put a curse on their beloved kingdom?

11. Give Jesse's reaction upon entering the National Art Gallery?

12. Which display in the Smithsonian is Jesse attracted to the most? Why?

13. Why does Brenda continue to question Jesse at breakfast Friday morning after Leslie had died?

14. Why does Jesse become angry while at the Burke's the Friday after Leslie's death? What does he do?

15. After milking Bessie Saturday morning where does Jesse go and why?

III. Essay

'This one perfect day of his life was worth anything he had to pay.' The author uses these words to describe Jesse's thrilling time at the museum with Miss Edmunds. Explain how this passage serves as foreshadowing for the upcoming tragedy.

Bridge to Terabithia Short Answer Unit Test 1 page 4

IV. Vocabulary

Listen to the vocabulary word and spell it. After you have spelled all the words, go back and write down the definitions.

1.

2.

3.

4.

5.

6.

7.

8.

9.

10.

KEY: SHORT ANSWER UNIT TEST #1 - *Bridge to Terabithia*

I. Matching/Identify

_F_	1. Paint Set	A. Leslie reigned as this over Terabithia
_A_	2. Queen	B. Worships Jesse
_B_	3. May Belle	C. Local elementary school
_H_	4. Lumber	D. Entry into secret kingdom
_C_	5. Lark Creek	E. Author
_K_	6. Janice Avery	F. Christmas gift from Leslie to Jesse
_G_	7. Guts	G. Jesse thinks he has none
_M_	8. Drowned	H. Used to build a bridge over creek bed
_E_	9. Paterson	I. Guardian of Terabithia
_J_	10. Easter	J. When Lelsie went to church with Jesse
_D_	11. Rope Swing	K. Seventh grade bully
_N_	12. Value Structure	L. Topic of Leslie's essay
_O_	13. TV	M. How Leslie died
_L_	14. Scuba Diving	N. Leslie's parents were reassessing theirs
_I_	15. Prince Terrien	O. Burke's have none

II. Short Answer

1. Who is Miss Julia Edmunds and why is she special to Jesse?
    She is the denim-clad hippie-type music teacher who thinks Jesse is unusually talented.

2. What kind of relationship do Jesse and his father have?
    Jesse longs for a closer relationship with his father who is gone from sun-up to late every night working in Washington.

3. What surprise occurs at recess?
    Leslie wants to run with the boys, which is unheard of at their school, **and** she beats them.

4. Why does the class give Leslie a hard time after Mrs. Myers assigns the TV program for homework?
    She admits to the teacher that her family has no TV.

5. How do Jesse's parents feel about his relationship with Leslie?
    They are worried that their only son dioes nothing but play with girls and worries about what will become of him.

6. Why does Jesse become angry when Brenda criticizes Leslie?
    He can't believe he is related to someone he thinks is as dumb as Brenda and that she would dare criticize Leslie, whom he respects more.

7. In what way do Leslie and Jesse feel differently about their parents?
    Leslie likes to relate to her parents: to understand them; while Jesse thinks parents are what they are, not something for you to try to puzzle out. He thinks there is something weird about a grown man wanting to be friends with his own child.

8. Jesse and Leslie go to the pine grove after returning to their kingdom after a month's absence. Why?
    They go to the sacred place to give thanks for their victory against the imaginary foe they defeated upon their return to their kingdom.

9. What Lark Creek Elementary rule had Janice broken?
    You never mix up troubles at home with life at school. By admitting her father was beating her, it was viewed that she had betrayed him.

10. On Wednesday why did Leslie think some evil being had put a curse on their beloved kingdom?
    While they were sitting in the castle, it began suddenly to rain so hard that the water came through the top of the shack in icy streams.

11. Give Jesse's reaction upon entering the National Art Gallery?
    It was like stepping into the pine grove- the huge vaulted marble, the cool splash of the fountain, and the green glowing all around. He felt drunk with the color, form, and hugeness.

12. Which display in the Smithsonian is Jesse attracted to the most? Why?
    He attracted to the display of the of a miniature scene of Indians disguised in buffalo skins scaring a herd of buffalo over a cliff to their death. It was a three-dimensional nightmare version of some of his own drawings. He felt a sense of kinship.

13. Why does Brenda continue to question Jesse at breakfast Friday morning?
    She can't believe he is sitting there gobbling down plates of pancakes instead of reacting to Leslie's death. He is in denial.

14. Why does Jesse become angry while at the Burke's? What does he do?
    When her dad tells Jesse she has been cremated he realizes he will never see her again and he is furious. He thinks they are all crying for themselves, not Leslie. He is mad enough to sock her dad, but runs off towards home. Upon reaching home, he hits May Belle in the face after she asks if he saw her laid out.

15. After milking Bessie Saturday morning where does Jesse go and why?
    He goes to the stream and finds a large tree branch that has washed up into the bank. He uses it to cross over into Terabithia. He then makes a funeral wreath out of a pine bough bent into a circle adorned with spring beauties from the forest floor. He and P. T. take it to the sacred pine grove and lay it on the thick carpet of golden needles and Jesse says : "Father, into Thy hands I commend her spirit." He felt Leslie would have approved of the words for they had the ring of the sacred grove in them.

III. Essay
   'This one perfect day of his life was worth anything he had to pay.' The author uses these words to describe Jesse's thrilling time at the museum with Miss Edmunds. Explain how this passage serves as foreshadowing for the upcoming tragedy.

IV. Vocabulary
   Choose ten of the vocabulary words to read orally for the vocabulary section of this unit test.

SHORT ANSWER UNIT TEST 2 *Bridge to Terabithia*

I. Matching/Identify

___ 1. Neat kid   A. Fastest runner in fifth grade

___ 2. Miss Edmunds   B. Refinished Burke house room

___ 3. Laid off   C. C. S. Lewis' magical kingdom

___ 4. Leslie   D. How Leslie addressed her parents

___ 5. First names   E. Delivers new people to old Perkins' place

___ 6. Fridays   F. Leslie's parents' jobs

___ 7. Miss Bessie   G. Jessie milks her daily

___ 8. Narnia   H. What Miss Edmund's calls Jesse

___ 9. U-Haul   I. Jesse's youngest sister

___ 10. Joyce Ann   J. Where Leslie's ashes were taken

___ 11. Golden Room   K. Miss Edmunds' instrument

___ 12. Rain   L. Evil curse

___ 13. Writers   M. This happened to Jesse's dad

___ 14. Pennsylvania   N. Peace-loving music teacher

___ 15. Guitar   O. Miss Edmund's day at Lark Creek

II. Short Answer

1. Who is Jesse Oliver Aarons, Jr. and why does he rise so early in the morning every day during summer vacation?

Bridge to Terabithia Short Answer Unit Test 2 Page 2

2. List the daughters in the Aarons' household from oldest to youngest. Which sister worships Jesse?

3. What is Jesse's favorite pastime?

4. What idea does Jesse have for his drawings during 'down time' the first day back at school?

5. When does Jesse finally decide to befriend Leslie?

6. What surprisingly courageous thing does Jesse do on the bus ride home the afternoon he smiled at Leslie during music class?

7. Where do Jesse and Leslie go and what do they call it?

8. What did Janice Avery do to May Belle? How do Jesse and Leslie seek revenge?

9. As Christmas nears, Jesse is getting more concerned. Why? How does he solve his problem?

Bridge to Terabithia Short Answer Unit Test 2 Page 3

10. Something happens to make Jess and Leslie feel sorry for Janice Avery. What? How do they help her?

11. What is the main point of disagreement between May Belle and Leslie on the way home from church?

12. Why did Jesse awake with a feeling of dread Wednesday night?

13. What does Jesse do after he is told about Leslie?

14. Where does he go after leaving the Burke's and for what?

15. Who shows up and what problem does she face? How does Jesse help her?

III. Essay (Use the back of this page)
Explain what you think Leslie was saying after her visit to church with the Aarons' on Easter Sunday. "It's crazy, isn't it? You have to believe it, but you hate it. I don't have to believe it, and I think it's beautiful. It's crazy."

Bridge to Terabithia Short Answer Unit Test 2 Page 4

IV. Vocabulary

Listen to the vocabulary words and spell them. After you have spelled all the words, go back and write down the definitions.

1.

2.

3.

4.

5.

6.

7.

8.

9.

10.

KEY: SHORT ANSWER UNIT TEST 2 *Bridge to Terabithia*

I. Matching

_H_	1. Neat kid	A. Fastest runner in fifth grade
_N_	2. Miss Edmunds	B. Refinished Burke house room
_M_	3. Laid off	C. C. S. Lewis' magical kingdom
_A_	4. Leslie	D. How Leslie addressed her parents
_D_	5. First names	E. Delivers new people to old Perkins' place
_O_	6. Fridays	F. Leslie's parents' jobs
_G_	7. Miss Bessie	G. Jessie milks her daily
_C_	8. Narnia	H. What Miss Edmund's calls Jesse
_E_	9. U-Haul	I. Jesse's youngest sister
_I_	10. Joyce Ann	J. Where Leslie's ashes were taken
_B_	11. Golden Room	K. Miss Edmunds' instrument
_L_	12. Rain	L. Evil curse
_F_	13. Writers	M. This happened to Jesse's dad
_J_	14. Pennsylvania	N. Peace-loving music teacher
_K_	15. Guitar	O. Miss Edmund's day at Lark Creek

II. Short Answer

1. Who is Jesse Oliver Aarons, Jr. and why does he rise so early in the morning every day during summer vacation?

    He is a long-legged ten-year-old boy in a family of all girls living in a Northern Virginia rural area. He gets up to practice running so he can be the fastest boy in fifth grade when school resumes.

2. List the daughters in the Aarons' household from oldest to youngest. Which sister worships Jesse?

    Ellie, Brenda, May Belle, and Joyce Ann. Jesse's six-year-old sister, May Belle, worships him.

3. What is Jesse's favorite pastime?

    Jesse draws the way some people drink.

4. What idea does Jesse have for his drawings during 'down time' the first day back at school?

    He wants to do a whole book of drawings with one chief animal character.

5. When does Jesse finally decide to befriend Leslie?

    Jesse is feeling delighted during Miss Edmunds' music class while they all sit on the floor. He decides to smile at Leslie and she smiles back.

6. What surprisingly courageous thing does Jesse do on the bus ride home the afternoon he smiled at Leslie during music class?

    He retrieves Leslie from the back of the bus where Janice Avery always sits and makes a rude comment to Janice on her way back to her seat so she won't pick on Leslie.

7. Where do Jesse and Leslie go and what do they call it?

    They find a rope hanging from a crab apple tree that swings across a creek bed. The creek bed separates the farmland from the woods. They decide to make a secret place, just for the two of them, just a few yards beyond the creek bed and swing. They call it Terabithia.

8. What did Janice Avery do to May Belle? How do Jesse and Leslie seek revenge?

    She stole May Belle's Twinkies. They plant a note in her desk supposedly written by a popular seventh grade boy professing his undying love for her and asking her to meet him after school

9. As Christmas nears, Jesse is getting more concerned. Why? How does he solve his problem?

    He doesn't have a Christmas present for Leslie yet. He sees a sign for free puppies while riding home on the bus and decides to hop off and get one for her.

10. Something happens to make Jesse and Leslie feel sorry for Janice Avery. What? How do they help her?

    Leslie overhears her crying in the girls' bathroom. Jesse insists they need to try to help her. Leslie is opposed but agrees to go into the girls' bathroom and try to talk to her.

11. What is the main point of disagreement between May Belle and Leslie on the way home from church?

May Belle says that God will damn you to hell when you die if you don't believe in the Bible. Leslie disagrees.

12. Why did Jesse awake with a feeling of dread Wednesday night?
    It was still raining and he knew he had to tell Leslie he wouldn't go to Terabithia. He didn't mind telling her as much as he minded being afraid to go.

13. What does Jesse do after he is told about Leslie?
    He yells that they are lying to him and runs out the door away from everything.

14. Where does he go after leaving the Burke's and for what?
    He retrieved the paints and paper Leslie had given him for Christmas from under his mattress, and takes them down to the stream and flings then into the dirty brown water.

15. Who shows up and what problem does she face? How does Jesse help her?
    May Belle has followed Jess and has gotten halfway across the tree bridge. She is terrified to move forwards or backwards. He inches out on the branch until he is close enough to touch her. He then tells her to back up and holding onto her, he guides her backwards to the home side of the bank.

III. Essay
    Explain what you think Leslie was saying after her visit to church with the Aarons' on Easter Sunday. "It's crazy, isn't it? You have to believe it, but you hate it. I don't have to believe it, and I think it's beautiful. It's crazy."

IV. Vocabulary
    Choose ten of the vocabulary words to read orally for the vocabulary section of the test.

ADVANCED SHORT ANSWER UNIT TEST - *Bridge to Terabithia*

I. Matching

___ 1. Neat kid   A. Fastest runner in fifth grade

___ 2. Miss Edmunds   B. Refinished Burke house room

___ 3. Laid off   C. C. S. Lewis' magical kingdom

___ 4. Leslie   D. How Leslie addressed her parents

___ 5. First names   E. Delivers new people to old Perkins' place

___ 6. Fridays   F. Leslie's parents' jobs

___ 7. Miss Bessie   G. Jessie milks her daily

___ 8. Narnia   H. What Miss Edmund's calls Jesse

___ 9. U-Haul   I. Jesse's youngest sister

___ 10. Joyce Ann   J. Where Leslie's ashes were taken

___ 11. Golden Room   K. Miss Edmunds' instrument

___ 12. Rain   L. Evil curse

___ 13. Writers   M. This happened to Jesse's dad

___ 14. Pennsylvania   N. Peace-loving music teacher

___ 15. Guitar   O. Miss Edmund's day at Lark Creek

II. Short Answer
1. Explain the significance of the title "*Bridge to Terabithia.*"

Bridge to Terabithia Advanced Short Answer Unit Test Page 2

2. Who is responsible for Leslie's death? Defend your answer.

3. "This one perfect day of his life was worth anything he had to pay." These were Jesse's thoughts on the way to Washington with Miss Edmunds. Why did the author include them?

4. Is the story of *Bridge to Terabithia* believable? Why or why not?

5. What was symbolic about the Indian/buffalo display at the Smithsonian that attracted Jesse?

6. Explain why the author included this statement of Leslie's after Easter Sunday church, "It's crazy, isn't it? You have to believe it, but you hate it. I don't have to believe it, and I think it's beautiful. It's crazy."

7. Will Jesse "pay back to the world in beauty and caring what Leslie loaned him in vision and strength" like he says? Support your answer.

Bridge to Terabithia Advanced Short Answer Unit Test Page 3

III. Quotations: Explain the importance and meaning of the following quotations.

1. "What are they teaching you in that damn school? Bunch of old ladies turning my only son into some kind of a-"

2. "You're the proverbial diamond in the rough."

3. "Sometimes like the Barbie doll you need to give people something that's for them, not just something that makes you feel good giving it."

4. "If she was an animal predator, we'd we obliged to help her."

5. "But Leslie, what if you die? What's going to happen to you if you die?.

6. "She had tricked him. She had made him leave is old self behind and come into her world, and then before he was really at home in it but too late to go back, she had left him stranded there- like an astronaut wandering about on the moon. Alone."

7. "It was Leslie who had taken him from the cow pasture into Terabithia and turned him into a king. He had thought that was it. Wasn't king the best you could be? Now it occurred to him that perhaps Terabithia was like a castle when you came to be knighted. After you stayed for a while and grew strong you had to move on. For hadn't Leslie, even in Terabithia, tried to push back the walls of his mind and make him see beyond to the shining world-huge and terrible and beautiful and very fragile?

Bridge to Terabithia Advanced Short Answer Unit Test Page 4

IV. Vocabulary
Listen to the vocabulary words and write them down. After you have written down all the words, write a paragraph in which you use all the words. The paragraph must in some way relate to *Bridge to Terabithia*.

MULTIPLE CHOICE UNIT TEST 1 - *Bridge to Terabithia*

I. Matching

1. _____ Neat kid   A. Jesse reigned as this over Terabithia

2. _____ King   B. Sacred place

3. _____ Judy and Bill   C. Jesse thinks he has none

4. _____ Easter   D. Secret kingdom entry

5. _____ Guts   E. Author

6. _____ Beans   F. When Leslie went to church for first time

7. _____ Paterson   G. What Miss Edmunds calls Jesse

8. _____ Rope Swing   H. Jesse milks her daily

9. _____ Pine Forest   I. Jesse needs to pick and can these

10. ____ Miss Bessie   J. Leslie's parents

II. Multiple Choice

1. Jesse rises extra early every day of summer vacation because
    a. he wants to improve his running time for the next school year.
    b. it is the only free time he has away from all his brothers and sisters.
    c. he hates sharing his room with two girls and gets up to sleep in the barn with a cow.
    d. he has to milk the family cow before anyone else arises.

2. Select the correct list of girls in Jesse's family going from eldest to youngest.
    a. Brenda, Ellie, Joyce Ann, May Belle
    b. Jessie, Joyce Ann, Brenda, Ellie
    c. Ellie, Leslie, Brenda, May Belle.
    d. Ellie, Brenda, May Belle, Joyce Ann.

3. Miss Julia Edmunds is
    a. the itinerant art teacher at Lark Creek.
    b. Lark Creek Elementary's music teacher.
    c. a teacher who thinks Jesse is unusually talented
    d. both b and c

Bridge to Terabithia Multiple Choice Unit Test 1 page 2

4. Jesse and his father
    a. work together and are very close.
    b. don't see much of each other.
    c. fight about Jessie's chores.
    d. spend hours fishing and talking over the weekends.

5. The big surprise at recess is
    a. The lower field is too muddy to run on due to the recent storm.
    b. The older boys are now racing each other.
    c. The gym teacher won't let the boys race because it is too close to phys ed. time.
    d. Leslie insists on running with the boys and beats them all.

6. Jesse finally decides to befriend Leslie when
    a. she keeps bugging him about it.
    b. they are on the bus and he no longer wants to sit with May Belle.
    c. they are in music class and he is in a delightful mood.
    d. she shows up in the barn to help him milk the cow.

7. Leslie's parents are
    a. highly educated.
    b. writers in designer jeans.
    c. straight- teethed and have lots of hair.
    d. all of the above

8. Jesse's parents worry what will happen to him because
    a. he spends all his time with a girl.
    b. he spends too much time fishing.
    c. he isn't doing well in school.
    d. he isn't doing the chores he is supposed to do.

9. Janice Avery stole
    a. Jesse's drawings.
    b. Leslie's paint set and paper.
    c. May Belle's Twinkie
    d. Brenda's boyfriend.

Bridge to Terabithia Multiple Choice Unit Test 1 page 3

10. When Brenda criticizes Leslie, Jesse
    a. smacks her in the face.
    b. becomes angry because he thinks more of Leslie than his own sister.
    c. tells their mother on her.
    d. throws his breakfast dish at her.

11. For Christmas Leslie gives Jesse
    a. watercolors
    b. brushes
    c. a pad of thick art paper
    d. all of the above

12. Jesse and Leslie go to the pine grove after returning to their kingdom to
    a. see if anything had changed.
    b. say the blessing of the pines.
    c. give thanks for their victory against the imaginary foe they defeated.
    d. look for a lost doe.

13. Janice Avery broke this rule:
    a. do unto others as you would have others do unto you.
    b. never tell someone you don't trust a secret.
    c. never mix up troubles from home with life at school.
    d. be friendly; all else will follow.

14. Where does Leslie ask to go that surprises Jesse?
    a. museum
    b. farm convention
    c. Millsburg
    d. church

15. Leslie and May Belle disagree about
    a. the church service they just left.
    b. Jesus dying on the cross.
    c. reading the Bible in a year.
    d. God damning to hell those that do not believe.

Bridge to Terabithia Multiple Choice Unit Test 1 page 4

16. Why did Leslie think some evil being had put a curse on their beloved kingdom?
    a. they could hear eerie noises coming from the castle.
    b. the rain came through the top of their castle in icy streams.
    c. the rain had washed their castle away.
    d. none of the above

17. Jesse awoke with a feeling of dread Wednesday night due to
    a. the unending rain.
    b. the fact that he is afraid to re-enter Terabithia while the creek is swollen.
    c. he knows he must tell Leslie he won't go.
    d. all of the above

18. When Jesse awakens in the middle of the night, he pushes away the falling sensation by
    a. reciting the Lord's Prayer.
    b. recalling and reciting the past day's events with Miss Edmunds, detail by detail.
    c. remembering everything Leslie ever told him.
    d. counting sheep.

19. Why does Jesse hit May Belle in the face?
    a. He was angry Leslie had been cremated.
    b. She was in his paints again.
    c. She asked the wrong thing at the wrong time.
    d. both a and c

20. Mrs. Myers calls Jesse into the hall because
    a. he didn't stand for the pledge of allegiance.
    b. she wants to express her sympathy to him over Leslie's death.
    c. she wants to share with him about her husband and son's deaths.
    d. he threw a tantrum about Leslie's seat being removed before he could touch it.

Bridge to Terabithia Multiple Choice Unit Test 1 page 5

III. Quotations: Identify the speaker:

A= Jesse B= Leslie C= May Bell D= Mr. Aarons
E= Miss Edmunds F= Mrs. Aarons G= Mrs. Myers

1. "All right, Jesse. Get your lazy self off that bench. Miss Bessie's bag is probably dragging to the ground by now. And you got beans to pick."

2. "What are they teaching you in that damn school? Bunch of old ladies turning my only son into some kind of a-"

3. "You're the proverbial diamond in the rough."

4. "Sometimes like the Barbie doll you need to give people something that's for them, not just something that makes you feel good giving it."

5. "My parents are reassessing their value structure."

6. "I am sure that all of you were as impressed as I was with Leslie's exciting essay."

7. "But Leslie, what if you die? What's going to happen to you if you die?.

8. "Then we'll name him Prince Terrien and make him the guardian of Terabithia."

9. "Hell, ain't it? Lord, boy, don't be a fool. God ain't gonna send any little girls to hell."

10. "She had tricked him. She had made him leave is old self behind and come into her world, and then before he was really at home in it but too late to go back, she had left him stranded there- like an astronaut wandering about on the moon. Alone.

Bridge to Terabithia Multiple Choice Unit Test 1 page 6

IV. Vocabulary (Matching)

___ 1. Consolation   A. Hopeless

___ 2. Faltered   B. Hating

___ 3. Solemn   C. Defeated

___ 4. Speculation   D. Comfort

___ 5. Cagey   E. Charge of guilt

___ 6. Ominously   F. Drenched; soaked

___ 7. Muddled   G. Hesitated; wavered

___ 8. Desperate   H. The whole thing

___ 9. Vile   I. Serious

___ 10. Insufficiencies   J. Consideration; thought

___ 11. Spectacle   K. Weaknesses

___ 12. Regally   L. Tricky; sly

___ 13. Crimson   M. Deep Red

___ 14. Exhilaration   N. Confused

___ 15. Revenge   O. Threateningly; darkly

___ 16. Shebang   P. Mean; disgusting

___ 17. Doused   Q. To get back at; punishment

___ 18. Vanquished   R. Public display

___ 19. Despising   S. Stately; dignified

___ 20. Accusation   T. Thrill

MULTIPLE CHOICE UNIT TEST 2 - *Bridge to Terabithia*

I. Matching

1. ____ Rain
2. ____ Joyce Ann
3. ____ Lark Creek
4. ____ Laid off
5. ____ Monster Mouth Myers
6. ____ Lumber
7. ____ Janice Avery
8. ____ Drawing
9. ____ Terabithia
10. ____ Arlington

A. Leslie's old school location
B. Secret kingdom
C. Jesse's youngest sister
D. Jesse's ability
E. Used to build bridge over creek bed
F. Fifth grade teacher
G. Evil curse
H. This happened to Jesse's dad
I. Seventh grade bully
J. Local elementary school

II. Multiple Choice

1. Jesse Oliver Aarons is
    a. a young girl from Washington D. C. who moves to Virginia.
    b. a ten-year-old boy in a family of all sisters.
    c. the fastest runner in third grade at Lark Creek Elementary.
    d. none of the above

2. The lower grade boys had started the races during recess because
    a. the older boys took the dry center of the upper field for their ball games.
    b. all the balls went to the upper grades.
    c. the girls claimed the small top section for hopscotch or jump rope.
    d. all of the above

3. Ellie and Brenda went
    a. school shopping with their mother.
    b. to the local swimming pool with the neighbors.
    c. shopping to Millsburg Plaza with the Timmons.
    d. roller skating with their boyfriends.

Bridge to Terabithia Short Answer Unit Test 2 Page 2

4. Which sister of Jessie's worships him?
    a. May Belle
    b. Brenda
    c. Joyce Ann
    d. Ellie

5. Miss Julia Edmunds is
    a. the itinerant art teacher at Lark Creek.
    b. Lark Creek Elementary's music teacher.
    c. a teacher who thinks Jesse is unusually talented
    d. both b and c

6. Jesse and his father
    a. work together and are very close.
    b. don't see much of each other.
    c. fight about Jessie's chores.
    d. spend hours fishing and talking over the weekends.

7. Jesse finally decides to befriend Leslie when
    a. she keeps bugging him about it.
    b. they are on the bus and he no longer wants to sit with May Belle.
    c. they are in music class and he is in a delightful mood.
    d. she shows up in the barn to help him milk the cow.

8. Mrs. Myers reads Leslie's essay on scuba diving to the class. What is Jesse's reaction?
    a. He feels sorry for her because the other good writers will snub her.
    b. He is jealous because no one around there has a hobby such as that.
    c. He is enthralled with it and feels as if he is drowning.
    d. He tells her to stop trying to be such a teacher's pet.

9. Leslie bribes May Belle so she and Jesse can spend the afternoon by themselves by giving her
    a. a baby doll that walks and talks.
    b. a pad of paper and a new box of crayons.
    c. some of her favorite candy.
    d. a brand new package of paper dolls.

Bridge to Terabithia Short Answer Unit Test 2 Page 3

10. Jesse's biggest problem before Christmas is
    a. he has no gift for Leslie.
    b. lack of money to buy May Belle's Barbie doll.
    c. how to tell Leslie he can't afford a gift for her.
    d. all of the above

11. Jesse's dad is unhappy on Christmas morning because
    a. the racing-car track isn't running properly.
    b. Jesse doesn't like his gift.
    c. the girls will not quit bickering.
    d. he couldn't afford to buy his children more expensive gifts for Christmas.

12. Leslie invites Jessie to
    a. help her and her father restore the house.
    b. come to Pennsylvania to visit her grandparents with her.
    c. go to Arlington to visit a friend.
    d. come to a New Year's dinner.

13. "The Golden Room" is a good name for chapter seven because
    a. the chapter is all about the myth of the goose and the golden egg.
    b. they couldn't decide whether to paint the room blue or gold.
    c. the chapter is about fixing-up the room they paint gold.
    d. they find gold beneath the old, black floor boards.

14. Jesse and Leslie help Janice Avery by
    a. taking her note to the boy she liked.
    b. beating up her friends.
    c. telling the teacher the nature of her problems.
    d. approaching her and listening to her problems.

15. Why did Leslie think some evil being had put a curse on their beloved kingdom?
    a. they could hear eerie noises coming from the castle.
    b. the rain came through the top of their castle in icy streams.
    c. the rain had washed their castle away.
    d. none of the above

Bridge to Terabithia Short Answer Unit Test 2 Page 4

16. Jesse awoke with a feeling of dread Wednesday night due to
    a. the unending rain.
    b. the fact that he is afraid to re-enter Terabithia while the creek is swollen.
    c. he knows he must tell Leslie he won't go.
    d. all of the above

17. Jesse's reaction upon entering the National Art Gallery was one of
    a. fear of all the crowds.
    b. drunkenness with the color, form, and hugeness.
    c. doubt of the authenticity of the art.
    d. none of the above

18. Brenda is upset with Jesse because he
    a. acts like he doesn't care about Leslie's death.
    b. is in denial.
    c. eats a couple of plates of pancakes.
    d. all of the above

19. What does Jesse do after he retrieves his paints and paper Leslie had given him?
    a. He burns them in the garbage pile.
    b. He flings them in the swollen stream.
    c. He gives them to May Belle.
    d. He gives them back to Leslie's parents.

20. May Belle now assumes the role of
    a. princess of the pine grove.
    b. queen of Terabithia.
    c. court jester of the kingdom.
    d. queen of the sacred place.

Bridge to Terabithia Multiple Choice Unit Test 1 page 5

III. Quotations: Identify the speaker:

A= Miss Edmunds   B= May Belle   C= Mrs. Aarons   D= Mr. Aarons
E=Mrs. Myers   F= Jesse   G= Leslie

1. "All right, Jesse. Get your lazy self off that bench. Miss Bessie's bag is probably dragging to the ground by now. And you got beans to pick."

2. "What are they teaching you in that damn school? Bunch of old ladies turning my only son into some kind of a-"

3. "You're the proverbial diamond in the rough."

4. "Sometimes like the Barbie doll you need to give people something that's for them, not just something that makes you feel good giving it."

5. "My parents are reassessing their value structure."

6. "I am sure that all of you were as impressed as I was with Leslie's exciting essay."

7. "But Leslie, what if you die? What's going to happen to you if you die?.

8. "Then we'll name him Prince Terrien and make him the guardian of Terabithia."

9. "Hell, ain't it? Lord, boy, don't be a fool. God ain't gonna send any little girls to hell."

10. "She had tricked him. She had made him leave is old self behind and come into her world, and then before he was really at home in it but too late to go back, she had left him stranded there- like an astronaut wandering about on the moon. Alone."

Bridge to Terabithia Multiple Choice Unit Test 2 page 6

IV. Vocabulary (Matching)

___ 1. Dread   A. Assigned; designated

___ 2. Constricting   B. Terror

___ 3. Relentlessly   C. Known to; tendency

___ 4. Despite   D. Self-satisfied

___ 5. Alcove   E. Abandoned infant

___ 6. Inclined   F. In spite of

___ 7. Prescribed   G. Remains

___ 8. Foundling   H. Chubby

___ 9. Dregs   I. Two-faced

___ 10. Complacent   J. On purpose; intentionally

___ 11. Garish   K. Backbone; toughness

___ 12. Regicide   L. Energetically

___ 13. Pudgy   M. Combined

___ 14. Hypocritical   N. Recessed opening

___ 15. Grit   O. Uproar

___ 16. Deliberately   P. Glaring; showy

___ 17. Consolidated   Q. Without stopping

___ 18. Pandemonium   R. The killing of a king

___ 19. Vigorously   S. Tightening

___ 20. Reluctant   T. Unwilling

ANSWER SHEET - *Bridge to Terabithia*
Multiple Choice Unit Tests

I. Matching	II. Multiple Choice	III. Quotes	IV. Vocabulary
1. ___	1. ___	1. ___	1. ___
2. ___	2. ___	2. ___	2. ___
3. ___	3. ___	3. ___	3. ___
4. ___	4. ___	4. ___	4. ___
5. ___	5. ___	5. ___	5. ___
6. ___	6. ___	6. ___	6. ___
7. ___	7. ___	7. ___	7. ___
8. ___	8. ___	8. ___	8. ___
9. ___	9. ___	9. ___	9. ___
10. ___	10. ___	10. ___	10. ___
	11. ___		11. ___
	12. ___		12. ___
	13. ___		13. ___
	14. ___		14. ___
	15. ___		15. ___
	16. ___		16. ___
	17. ___		17. ___
	18. ___		18. ___
	19. ___		19. ___
	20. ___		20. ___

ANSWER KEY MULTIPLE CHOICE UNIT TESTS – *Bridge to Terabithia*

Answers to Unit Test 1 are in the left column. Answers to Unit Test 2 are in the right column.

I. Matching	II. Multiple Choice	III. Quotes	IV. Vocabulary
1. G G	1. A B	1. F C	1. D B
2. A C	2. D D	2. D D	2. G S
3. J J	3. D C	3. E A	3. I Q
4. F H	4. B A	4. A F	4. J F
5. C F	5. D D	5. B G	5. L N
6. I E	6. C B	6. G E	6. O C
7. E I	7. D C	7. C B	7. N A
8. D D	8. A C	8. B G	8. A E
9. B B	9. C D	9. D D	9. P G
10. H A	10. B A	10. A F	10. K D
	11. D A		11. R P
	12. C A		12. S R
	13. C C		13. M H
	14. D D		14. T I
	15. D B		15. Q K
	16. B D		16. H J
	17. D B		17. F M
	18. B D		18. C O
	19. D B		19. B L
	20. A B		20. E T

UNIT RESOURCE MATERIALS

BULLETIN BOARD IDEAS - *Bridge to Terabithia*

1. Post students Writing Assignment #1, Want Ad Posters advertising for a friend.

2. Bring in (or have students bring in) pictures of castles, kingdoms, moats, drawbridges, etc. Make a collage if you have enough different pictures (or post individual pictures on colorful paper if you only have a few pictures). This could also be a fun introductory activity if students participate. You could have the border and title done for the bulletin board and invite students to staple up their own pictures wherever they want them. It will only take a few minutes of class time, but the students will enjoy it and you can get your bulletin board done in a hurry.

3. Draw one of the word search puzzles onto the bulletin board. (Be sure to enlarge it.) Write the key words to one side. Invite students to take their pens or markers and find the words before and/or after class (or perhaps this could be an activity for students who finish their work early).

4. Post information regarding nearby art galleries. If there are none nearby- display brochures from highly recognizable ones. Perhaps students could select a favorite portrait and artist and display their impression of it.

5. Portray artistic requirements of an artist and next to the pictures have students explain their function.

6. Illustrate Leslie and Jesse by either silhouettes, portraits, or whatever your choice. Include information gained from the novel describing them.

7. Post lyrics of the songs Jesse mentions are Miss Edmunds' favorites. Include the musical score. Have students illustrate the meaning of the lyrics. See page 13 in the novel.

8. Make a mural depicting Terabithia. Be sure to include the swing rope, the creek bed, the castle, and the pine grove.

9. Post any of the students' Writing Assignments, in addition to their Want Ads. They could illustrate something from their Writing Assignment to enhance it.

10. Create a collage of art work from students that conveys their impressions of the characters in this story.

EXTRA ACTIVITIES - *Bridge to Terabithia*

One of the difficulties in teaching a novel is that all students don't read at the same speed. One student who likes to read may take the book home and finish it in a day or two. Sometimes a few students finish the in-class assignments early. The problem, then, is finding suitable extra activities for students.

One thing you can do is to keep a little library in the classroom. For this unit on *Bridge to Terabithia*, you might check out from the school library other books by Katherine Paterson. A biography of the author would be interesting for some students. C. S. Lewis' Chronicles of Narnia may be of interest. You may include other related books and articles about: friendship, running, large families, artists, art, art galleries, castles, the Renaissance, northern Virginia, Washington D. C., political writing, Post Vietnam Era, Seventies Pop Culture, death, etc.

Other things you may keep on hand are puzzles. We have made some relating directly to *Bridge to Terabithia* for you. Feel free to duplicate them.

Some students may like to draw. You might devise a contest or allow some extra-credit grade for students who draw characters or scenes from *Bridge to Terabithia*. Note, too, that if the students do not want to keep their drawings you may pick up some extra bulletin board materials this way. If you have a contest and you supply the prize or, you could possibly make the drawing itself a non-refundable entry fee.

The pages which follow contain games, puzzles and worksheets. The keys, when appropriate, immediately follow the puzzle or worksheet. There are two main groups of activities: one group for the unit; that is, generally relating to the *Bridge to Terabithia* text, and another group of activities related strictly to the *Bridge to Terabithia* vocabulary.

Directions for the games, puzzles and worksheets are self-explanatory. The object here is to provide you with extra materials you may use in any way you choose.

MORE ACTIVITIES - *Bridge to Terabithia*

1. Pick a chapter or scene with a great deal of dialogue and have the students act it out on a stage. (Perhaps you could assign various scenes to different groups of students so more than one scene could be acted and more students could participate.)

2. Research and display materials an artist needs. Invite local artists into your class to inform them about this career option. Perhaps they could demonstrate their craft or hold a hands-on session. If no luck with local artist, ask your art teacher to help you out.

3. Have students design a book cover (front and back and inside flaps) for *Bridge to Terabithia*.

4. Students could write epitaphs for Leslie.

5. Debate the effects of a parents' disapproval of a child's abilities if they are different than theirs. For example, Jesse's father did not understand Jesse's artistic abilities and made derogatory remarks about what they were teaching his son....

6. Use some of the related topics (noted earlier for an in-class library) as topics for research, reports or written papers, or as topics for guest speakers.

7. Have students plan and teach a lesson on a chapter or section of the book. Give them guidelines and a time-frame.

8. Visit a Renaissance Fair.

9. Locate the lyrics to the songs Jesse mentions from the Seventies. Play recordings of them or actually perform them with a student pianist or other instrumentalist. Research their significance to this era. Those mentioned are "My Beautiful Balloon" (Fifth Dimension), "This Land is Your Land" (Peter, Paul, and Mary),"Free to Be You and Me" (Marlo Thomas), and "Blowing in the Wind" (Bob Dylan).

10. Write to Katherine Paterson asking her questions students have composed. You could send a class set of letters in one large envelope.

11. Construct a model of Leslie's and Jesse's Terabithia. Allow students to use it as a get-a-way to read quietly or reflect.

12. Research music, fashions, hairstyles, political sentiments, etc. of this era. Perhaps your students could research these topics and make a report to the class. This will help them better understand Miss Edmunds character.

More Activities - *Bridge to Terabithia* page 2

13. Visit an art gallery. If feasible visit the two mentioned in the book. The National Art Gallery and The Smithsonian in Washington D.C. If not feasible, write to them for information and report to the class.

14. Invite a willing relative of your students in to share information about this time period, perhaps a Vietnam veteran.

15. Have students interview someone who lived during this time period (Post Vietnam Era), preferably a parent. Have students compose questions together for their interviews. They could then make a booklet with the information in it for display. Have them illustrate the cover with something they learned about the times from their interview.

16. Allow students to select a character from the novel. Have them dress like them, speak like them; assume their persona. Create a talk show format with these characters as the guests. Have a student volunteer be the host. Others not involved will be the audience, questioning the characters. One of your students could pretend to be a trained psychologist who comes out later in the show to help the panel solve their problems. Have a topic like: sibling rivalry, i.e. problems encountered in the novel. Allow the class to decide as much as possible. Have questions from the audience ready prior to the show day. You could have students try out for the parts. Remind them to keep it on the up and up, not to mimic some of the seedier talk shows. This will require students to take an in-depth look into characterization in the novel.

17. View a filmstrip on Katherine Paterson.

18. Students who like board games may want to create one using information from this novel. Some students could work together as a group to complete this task. Encourage them to look at setting to illustrate their board and possibly use vocabulary, characters, plot, etc. for question cards.

19. Find out more about the concept Jesse saw illustrated at the Smithsonian about the Indians disguising themselves to trick the buffalo to jump off the cliff.

20. Research the practice of cremation.

21. Invite a freelance writer in to discuss his/her vocation. Ask them to be prepared to tell how they got started, their hours, etc. Later, compare to Leslie's parents' jobs.

PROJECT BUILD A BRIDGE

This project is an open-ended one. I think it is important for your students to come to some conclusion about what the meaning of the title is, to them personally. Spend as much time as possible, discussing various possibilities. Of course there is the obvious, literal meaning of the lumber bridge Jesse builds across the stream to Terabithia. But what deeper meaning can be found within that passage? What wonderful, new awareness and insight has Jesse gained by having known Leslie and allowing her imagination to take him places he never could have imagined? Are there some family relationships that have improved throughout the course of this novel that can somehow be linked to a bridge of some sort? Has a bridge been spanned in Jesse's quest for self-knowledge of his sensitivities and abilities?

This topic will require much thought and discussion, perhaps you would rather not tackle it. Exploring these types of symbols can be quite enlightening when done in an open, accepting environment where all possibilities are accepted and acknowledged.

Once your students have individually determined their judgments regarding this passage, ask them to portray this meaning in some sort of project or image. Maybe a few students would like to work together to demonstrate or role play their interpretation. Another student or group may want to construct a simple bridge and somehow make it show their meaning. I stand amazed at the depth of what students can come up with when given the opportunity. Some will need much assistance and encouragement to take that leap. Good luck and keep an open mind! I would not make it an extensive representation, just something simple to get their meaning across. Display if possible.

"It was Leslie who had taken him from the cow pasture into Terabithia and turned him into a king. He had thought that was it. Wasn't king the best you could be? Now it occurred to him that perhaps Terabithia was like a castle when you came to be knighted. After you stayed for a while and grew strong you had to move on. For hadn't Leslie, even in Terabithia, tried to push back the walls of his mind and make him see beyond to the shining world-huge and terrible and beautiful and very fragile?

WORD SEARCH - *Bridge to Terabithia*

All the words in this list are associated with *Bridge to Terabithia*. The words are placed backwards, forward, diagonally, up and down. The included words are listed below the word search.

```
T H I R T Y O N E Q B F R I D A Y S L E S L I E
K S L G D F E G B C F R X K N R A B S N L J T S
V W E U U E K M W O I J E D T I O U V G S L C S
Y A J R U T H K D Z R N N N G Q O W T D S W I W
S B L Q O N S I G N I W A R D L H S N N D R B E
D J G U E F A C R H F M O J B A R U P E E D L Y
A O M D E L Y D J W L E H P E E M Z T B D C G D
Z R L S X G J C Z X G Q G I T D X P M S H L V G
Q O L L U Z V T Z X X P B I E N A U B J T P Y T
G G X I S P F P L W V R R N Y I L V X E J V Y V
G M T C N J O Y C E A W H W N Z M F P Q A P F T
R A C I N G S C U B A P A T E R S O N A R N I A
R N L Y J C T F J L E Q B M F T R Z N J S P S J
R R I L H M L O Q E U S K V V I A B H S P R Q F
R K T A E A Q W N T S A S I M P F E V R T P R H
C N E I R R E T V W A S H I N G T O N T G E W G
R P G K M A Y F I R S T E U E G E A S T E R R D
```

ARLINGTON	FIRST	KING	RAIN
BARBIE	FOREST	LAIDOFF	ROPE
BEANS	FREE	LARK	SCUBA
BESSIE	FRIDAYS	LESLIE	TERRIEN
BLOUSE	GALLERY	LUMBER	THIRTYONE
BRENDA	GEORGIA	MAY	TV
DOLLS	GOLDEN	MONSTER	UHAUL
DRAWING	GUITAR	NARNIA	VALUE
DROWNED	GUTS	NEAT	WASHINGTON
EASTER	JANICE	PAINT	WRITERS
EDMUNDS	JESSE	PATERSON	
ELLIE	JOYCE	QUEEN	
FIFTH	JUDY	RACING	

KEY: WORD SEARCH - *Bridge to Terabithia*

All the words in this list are associated with *Bridge to Terabithia*. The words are placed backwards, forward, diagonally, up and down. The included words are listed below the word search.

```
        T H I R T Y O N E   B F R I D A Y S L E S L I E
          S   G D   E     C F R     R A   S     L
        V   E U U E       O I   E     I O U     S L
          A J R U T     D   N   N G   O W   D     I
            L Q O N S I G N I W A R D L   S N     R   E
        D     U E F A         O J B A R U     E E
        A O   D E L         E   E E M     B D
            R L   G       G     I T D   P M
            O L L U           B I E   A U B
          G   I S             R R   I L       E
          G   T N J O Y C E A W H   N   M   P   A
        R A C I N G S C U B A P A T E R S O N A R N I A
        R N L     T     J L E       F T   N         S
            I L     L O   E U S K     I A     S         F
              A E A   N   S A S I     F E     T       R
          N E I R R E T V W A S H I N G T O N       E
            K M A Y F I R S T E U E G E A S T E R R
```

ARLINGTON	FIRST	KING	RAIN
BARBIE	FOREST	LAIDOFF	ROPE
BEANS	FREE	LARK	SCUBA
BESSIE	FRIDAYS	LESLIE	TERRIEN
BLOUSE	GALLERY	LUMBER	THIRTYONE
BRENDA	GEORGIA	MAY	TV
DOLLS	GOLDEN	MONSTER	UHAUL
DRAWING	GUITAR	NARNIA	VALUE
DROWNED	GUTS	NEAT	WASHINGTON
EASTER	JANICE	PAINT	WRITERS
EDMUNDS	JESSE	PATERSON	
ELLIE	JOYCE	QUEEN	
FIFTH	JUDY	RACING	

CROSSWORD - *Bridge to Terabithia*

CROSSWORD CLUES - *Bridge to Terabithia*

ACROSS

1. Refinished room of the Burke's; ____ room
3. Jesse milks her daily; Miss ____
6. Jesse needs to pick and can these
9. Leslie's old school
12. Burke's have none
13. Miss Edmunds' instrument
14. Organ used for hearing
15. Local elementary school; ____ Creek
17. Evil curse
18. Neither's partner
19. Jesse's youngest sister; ____ Ann
20. Peace-loving music teacher; Miss ____
24. Negative reply
25. What Miss Edmunds calls Jesse; ____ Kid
26. Miss Edmunds' favorite song; --- to Be You and Me
28. Used to build bridge over creek bed
31. Entry into secret kingdom; ____ swing
33. How Leslie died
34. Miss Edmunds' day at Lark Creek
36. Solar energy is given by the ___
37. Opposite of more
38. Number of students in the fifth-grade class
39. Jesse thinks he has none

DOWN

1. Mrs. Aarons' homeplace
2. Fastest runner in the fifth grade
3. Eighth grade Aarons daughter
4. Topic of Leslie's essay; ____ diving
5. Leslie wanted to go to church with Jesse then
7. Eldest Aarons daughter
8. May Belle's beloved Christmas gift
10. Magical kingdom in C. S. Lewis stories
11. Guardian of Terabithia; Prince ____
15. What happened to Jesse's dad (2 words)
16. Jesse reigned as this over their kingdom
17. Jesse's Christmas gift from his dad; ___ car set
19. Seventh grade bully; ____ Avery
21. Worships Jesse; ___ Belle
22. Day trip Miss Edmunds and Jesse take; Nat'l. Art ____
23. Ten-year-old boy in family of all girls
27. Jesse's favorite pastime
29. Ellie's purchase in Millsburg; see-through ____
30. Sacred place; Pine ____
32. Unusual; peculiar
33. Bribe May Belle took; paper ____
34. Opposite of skinny
35. Paintings, drawings are known as ___

CROSSWORD - *Bridge to Terabithia*

MATCHING QUIZ/WORK SHEET 1 - *Bridge to Terabithia*

___ 1. Monster Mouth Myers   A. Used to build bridge over creek bed

___ 2. Judy and Bill   B. Where Leslie's ashes are taken

___ 3. Arlington   C. How Leslie dies

___ 4. Janice Avery   D. Worships Jesse

___ 5. Paper dolls   E. Eighth-grade sister of Jesse

___ 6. Easter   F. Fifth-grade teacher

___ 7. Brenda   G. Secret kingdom in C. S. Lewis books

___ 8. Georgia   H. Refinished room by the Burke's

___ 9. Free To Be You and Me   I. Jesse's Christmas present from his dad

___ 10. See-through blouse   J. Former school of Leslie's

___ 11. Pennsylvania   K. Leslie's parents

___ 12. Lumber   L. Seventh grade bully

___ 13. Drowned   M. Mrs. Aarons' home place

___ 14. May Belle   N. Miss Edmunds' favorite song

___ 15. Golden room   O. Miss Edmunds' day at Lark Creek

___ 16. Paterson   P. Bribe May Belle took

___ 17. Neat-kid   Q. When Leslie went to church with the Aarons

___ 18. Narnia   R. What Miss Edmunds' calls Jesse

___ 19. Race-car track   S. Ellie's purchase at Millsburg Plaza

___ 20. Fridays   T. Author of novel

KEY: MATCHING QUIZ/WORK SHEET 1 - *Bridge to Terabithia*

_F_ 1. Monster Mouth Myers		A. Used to build bridge over creek bed
_K_ 2. Judy and Bill		B. Where Leslie's ashes are taken
_J_ 3. Arlington		C. How Leslie dies
_L_ 4. Janice Avery		D. Worships Jesse
_P_ 5. Paper dolls		E. Eighth-grade sister of Jesse
_Q_ 6. Easter		F. Fifth-grade teacher
_E_ 7. Brenda		G. Secret kingdom in C. S. Lewis books
_M_ 8. Georgia		H. Refinished room by the Burke's
_N_ 9. Free To Be You and Me		I. Jesse's Christmas present from his dad
_S_ 10. See-through blouse		J. Former school of Leslie's
_B_ 11. Pennsylvania		K. Leslie's parents
_A_ 12. Lumber		L. Seventh grade bully
_C_ 13. Drowned		M. Mrs. Aarons' home place
_D_ 14. May Belle		N. Miss Edmunds' favorite song
_H_ 15. Golden room		O. Miss Edmunds' day at Lark Creek
_T_ 16. Paterson		P. Bribe May Belle took
_R_ 17. Neat-kid		Q. When Leslie went to church with the Aarons
_G_ 18. Narnia		R. What Miss Edmunds' calls Jesse
_I_ 19. Race-car track		S. Ellie's purchase at Millsburg Plaza
_O_ 20. Fridays		T. Author of novel

MATCHING QUIZ/WORKSHEET 2 - *Bridge to Terabithia*

___ 1. U-Haul   A. Peace-loving music teacher

___ 2. Miss Bessie   B. Miss Edmunds' instrument

___ 3. Lark Creek   C. Local elementary school

___ 4. Guts   D. Youngest daughter in the Aarons' family

___ 5. Miss Edmunds   E. Delivers new folks to the old Perkins' place

___ 6. Beans   F. Topic of Leslie's essay

___ 7. Guitar   G. What Leslie calls her parents by

___ 8. Drawing   H. This happened to Mr. Aarons

___ 9. Scuba diving   I. Jesse needs to pick and can

___ 10. National Art Gallery J. Jessie milks daily

___ 11. First names   K. Burke's family has none

___ 12. Prince Terrein   L. Secret kingdom

___ 13. Terabithia   M. Leslie's parents' jobs

___ 14. Joyce Ann   N. Evil curse

___ 15. Laid off   O. May Belle's beloved Christmas gift

___ 16. TV   P. Jesse thinks he has none

___ 17. Writers   Q. Jesse's favorite pastime

___ 18. Rain   R. Sacred place

___ 19. Pine forest   S. Guardian of Terabithia

___ 20. Barbie   T. Day trip for Miss Edmunds and Jesse

KEY: MATCHING QUIZ/WORKSHEET 2 - *Bridge to Terabithia*

_E_ 1. U-Haul	A.	Peace-loving music teacher
_J_ 2. Miss Bessie	B.	Miss Edmunds' instrument
_C_ 3. Lark Creek	C.	Local elementary school
_P_ 4. Guts	D.	Youngest daughter in the Aarons' family
_A_ 5. Miss Edmunds	E.	Delivers new folks to the old Perkins' place
_I_ 6. Beans	F.	Topic of Leslie's essay
_B_ 7. Guitar	G.	What Leslie calls her parents by
_Q_ 8. Drawing	H.	This happened to Mr. Aarons
_F_ 9. Scuba diving	I.	Jesse needs to pick and can
_T_ 10. National Art Gallery	J.	Jessie milks daily
_G_ 11. First names	K.	Burke's family has none
_S_ 12. Prince Terrein	L.	Secret kingdom
_L_ 13. Terabithia	M.	Leslie's parents' jobs
_D_ 14. Joyce Ann	N.	Evil curse
_H_ 15. Laid off	O.	May Belle's beloved Christmas gift
_K_ 16. TV	P.	Jesse thinks he has none
_M_ 17. Writers	Q.	Jesse's favorite pastime
_N_ 18. Rain	R.	Sacred place
_R_ 19. Pine forest	S.	Guardian of Terabithia
_O_ 20. Barbie	T.	Day trip for Miss Edmunds and Jesse

JUGGLE LETTER REVIEW GAME CLUE SHEET - *Bridge to Terabithia*

SCRAMBLED	WORD	CLUE
LINGONART	ARLINGTON	Leslie's old school
RBIEBA	BARBIE	May Belle's beloved Christmas gift
BENSA	BEANS	Jesse needs to pick and can these
NDABRE	BRENDA	Eighth grade Aarons daughter
AWNGDRI	DRAWING	Jesse's favorite pastime
OWDNEDR	DROWNED	How Leslie died
LIEEL	ELLIE	Eldest Aarons daughter
IDAFSRY	FRIDAYS	Miss Edmunds' day at Lark Creek
EORGIAG	GEORGIA	Mrs. Aarons' home place
DGOLOOMENR	GOLDEN ROOM	Refinished room of the Burke's
UIARGT	GUITAR	Miss Edmunds' instrument
UTSG	GUTS	Jesse thinks he has none
SEJES	JESSE	Ten-year-old boy in family of all girls
NGKI	KING	Jesse reigned as this over their kingdom
LAFIDOF	LAID OFF	What happened to Jesse's dad
REKCLAEKR	LARK CREEK	Local elementary school
SLILEE	LESLIE	Fastest runner in the fifth grade
BLERUM	LUMBER	Used to build bridge over creek bed
LLEAYBEM	MAY BELLE	Worships Jesse
SSBEMISSIE	MISS BESSIE	Jesse milks her daily
IAARNN	NARNIA	Magical kingdom in C. S. Lewis stories
NEIDATK	NEAT KID	What Miss Edmunds calls Jesse
AINTSPET	PAINT SET	Christmas gift to Jesse from Leslie
PAOLLSPERD	PAPER DOLLS	Bribe May Belle took
TERSPAON	PATERSON	Author
NSNIAYLPENVA	PENNSYLVANIA	Where Leslie's ashes were taken
PIRESTNEFO	PINE FOREST	Sacred place
INCPRETERRIEN	PRINCE TERRIEN	Guardian of Terabithia
UEQEN	QUEEN	Leslie reigned as this over Terabithia
AIRN	RAIN	Evil curse
SINUBCIVADG	SCUBA DIVING	Topic of Leslie's essay
EBITATIARH	TERABITHIA	Secret place
WTERSRI	WRITERS	Leslie's parents' jobs

VOCABULARY RESOURCE MATERIALS

VOCABULARY WORD SEARCH - *Bridge to Terabithia*

All the words in this list are associated with *Bridge to Terabithia* with emphasis on the vocabulary words being studied in the unit. The words are placed backwards, forward, diagonally, up and down. The included words are listed below the word search.

```
V I L E V O C L A R E G A L L Y R E G I C I D E
M K R F W V Q R S H E B A N G X G S J O J E E G
G U T E L Q G D I B V P X N Q V O D M D V T N S
T N I M L J D G S M T S E Z S L P M U E I I U S
O M I N O U S L Y V S E G N E V E R I P S L T X
P Y M G O U C A Y Q D O R M T N S R S I P E R G
I V D Y D M R T N L M E N T D E T E P R P E D H
F N I E V E E N A C G Y T Q R E D S U A L E F P
Q O C G S P R D I N T N S A R A E S R E R G A C
M K U L O P I D N N T U I R D D I A N E V R P C
B U K N I R E T N A G Y A T O I P T T D A B D P
J Q D V D N O R E R P Y J R A T L L O M C O R P
G W K D Y L E U A O K W E J Y E A O E R U S D R
F G R F L C I D S T U S X G S F S D S S O A K L
D Y R Q S E M N N L E S W S A L I U E N E U X Q
O B L I G E D W G G Y Y L L A C I D A R O P S M
B H D J T G A R I S H Y L Y S G E R D N P C M C
```

ALCOVE	DREDGING	OMINOUSLY	REPENTED
CAGEY	DREGS	PANDEMONIUM	RETRIEVED
COMMEND	FALTERED	PARAMEDICS	REVENGE
CONSOLIDATED	FOUNDLING	PARAPETS	SANCTUARY
CRIMSON	GARISH	PITEOUSLY	SHEBANG
DESPERATE	GRIT	PREDATORS	SOLEMN
DESPISING	INCLINED	PUDGY	SPORADICALLY
DESPITE	MOURNING	REGALLY	SURPLUS
DISCERN	MUDDLED	REGICIDE	TRAITOROUS
DOUSED	NAUSEATINGLY	RELENTLESSLY	VIGOROUSLY
DREAD	OBLIGED	RELUCTANT	VILE

KEY: VOCABULARY WORD SEARCH - *Bridge to Terabithia*

All the words in this list are associated with *Bridge to Terabithia* with emphasis on the vocabulary words being studied in the unit. The words are placed backwards, forward, diagonally, up and down. The included words are listed below the word search.

```
V I L E V O C L A R E G A L L Y R E G I C I D E
M   R         R S H E B A N G     G S   O     E E G
G U   E         I     P           O D M     V T N S
  N I M L         M       E       L   M U E I I U S
O M I N O U S L Y     S E G N E V E R I P S L T
      G O U C A Y     D O   M T N     R S I P E R
I V D     D M R T N L   E N T D E T E P R P E D
F N I E   E E N A C G   T   R E D S U A L E       P
  O C G S P R D I N T N S A R A E S R E R     A
M   U L O P I D N N T U I R D D I A N E       R
    U   N I R E T N A G   A T O I P T T     A   D
      D   D N O R E     P Y   R A T L L O M     O
        D   L E U A O       E   Y E A O E R U   D
        G     L C I D S T U     G S F S D S S O A
        R   S E   N   L E S     S A   I U E N E U
O B L I G E D   G   Y Y L L A C I D A R O P S
        D   T G A R I S H Y   Y S G E R D N P C
```

ALCOVE	DREDGING	OMINOUSLY	REPENTED
CAGEY	DREGS	PANDEMONIUM	RETRIEVED
COMMEND	FALTERED	PARAMEDICS	REVENGE
CONSOLIDATED	FOUNDLING	PARAPETS	SANCTUARY
CRIMSON	GARISH	PITEOUSLY	SHEBANG
DESPERATE	GRIT	PREDATORS	SOLEMN
DESPISING	INCLINED	PUDGY	SPORADICALLY
DESPITE	MOURNING	REGALLY	SURPLUS
DISCERN	MUDDLED	REGICIDE	TRAITOROUS
DOUSED	NAUSEATINGLY	RELENTLESSLY	VIGOROUSLY
DREAD	OBLIGED	RELUCTANT	VILE

VOCABULARY CROSSWORD - *Bridge to Terabithia*

VOCABULARY CROSSWORD CLUES - *Bridge to Terabithia*

ACROSS
1. Chubby
2. Comfort
8. Sickeningly
10. Meowing animal
12. Opposite of beginning
13. Bottom part of a flower
14. Purchase
15. The killing of a king
16. Twelve o'clock
17. Remains
18. Backbone
23. Dirt
24. Sight organ
25. Told an untruth
26. Mean; disgusting
27. Not difficult
29. Either's partner
30. Hesitated; wavered
32. Building where people live
34. Drenched; soaked
35. Barriers
36. Affirmative reply
37. Extra amount

DOWN
1. Uproar
2. Deep red
3. Serious
4. Recessed opening
5. Drunk
6. Confused
7. Tricky; sly
9. The whole thing
11. Sissified manner
15. Stately; dignified
17. Hopeless
19. To get back at; punishment
20. Disloyal; back-stabbing
21. Energetically
22. Threateningly; darkly
28. Terror
31. Pull behind you on the ground
33. Opposite of dry

VOCABULARY CROSSWORD - *Bridge to Terabithia*

VOCABULARY WORK SHEET 1 - *Bridge to Terabithia*

___ 1. Consolation   A. Hopeless

___ 2. Faltered   B. Hating

___ 3. Solemn   C. Defeated

___ 4. Speculation   D. Comfort

___ 5. Cagey   E. Charge of guilt

___ 6. Ominously   F. Drenched; soaked

___ 7. Muddled   G. Hesitated; wavered

___ 8. Desperate   H. The whole thing

___ 9. Vile   I. Serious

___ 10. Insufficiencies   J. Consideration; thought

___ 11. Spectacle   K. Weaknesses

___ 12. Regally   L. Tricky; sly

___ 13. Crimson   M. Deep Red

___ 14. Exhilaration   N. Confused

___ 15. Revenge   O. Threateningly; darkly

___ 16. Shebang   P. Mean; disgusting

___ 17. Doused   Q. To get back at; punishment

___ 18. Vanquished   R. Public display

___ 19. Despising   S. Stately; dignified

___ 20. Accusation   T. Thrill

KEY: VOCABULARY WORKSHEET 1 - *Bridge to Terabithia*

D	1. Consolation	A.	Hopeless
G	2. Faltered	B.	Hating
I	3. Solemn	C.	Defeated
J	4. Speculation	D.	Comfort
L	5. Cagey	E.	Charge of guilt
O	6. Ominously	F.	Drenched; soaked
N	7. Muddled	G.	Hesitated; wavered
A	8. Desperate	H.	The whole thing
P	9. Vile	I.	Serious
K	10. Insufficiencies	J.	Consideration; thought
R	11. Spectacle	K.	Weaknesses
S	12. Regally	L.	Tricky; sly
M	13. Crimson	M.	Deep Red
T	14. Exhilaration	N.	Confused
Q	15. Revenge	O.	Threateningly; darkly
H	16. Shebang	P.	Mean; disgusting
F	17. Doused	Q.	To get back at; punishment
C	18. Vanquished	R.	Public display
B	19. Despising	S.	Stately; dignified
E	20. Accusation	T.	Thrill

VOCABULARY WORKSHEET 2 - *Bridge to Terabithia*

___ 1. Dread   A. Assigned; designated

___ 2. Constricting   B. Terror

___ 3. Relentlessly   C. Known to; tendency

___ 4. Despite   D. Self-satisfied

___ 5. Alcove   E. Abandoned infant

___ 6. Inclined   F. In spite of

___ 7. Prescribed   G. Remains

___ 8. Foundling   H. Chubby

___ 9. Dregs   I. Two-faced

___ 10. Complacent   J. On purpose; intentionally

___ 11. Garish   K. Backbone; toughness

___ 12. Regicide   L. Energetically

___ 13. Pudgy   M. Combined

___ 14. Hypocritical   N. Recessed opening

___ 15. Grit   O. Uproar

___ 16. Deliberately   P. Glaring; showy

___ 17. Consolidated   Q. Without stopping

___ 18. Pandemonium   R. The killing of a king

___ 19. Vigorously   S. Tightening

___ 20. Reluctant   T. Unwilling

KEY: VOCABULARY WORKSHEET 2 - *Bridge to Terabithia*

B	1. Dread	A. Assigned; designated
S	2. Constricting	B. Terror
Q	3. Relentlessly	C. Known to; tendency
F	4. Despite	D. Self-satisfied
N	5. Alcove	E. Abandoned infant
C	6. Inclined	F. In spite of
A	7. Prescribed	G. Remains
E	8. Foundling	H. Chubby
G	9. Dregs	I. Two-faced
D	10. Complacent	J. On purpose; intentionally
P	11. Garish	K. Backbone; toughness
R	12. Regicide	L. Energetically
H	13. Pudgy	M. Combined
I	14. Hypocritical	N. Recessed opening
K	15. Grit	O. Uproar
J	16. Deliberately	P. Glaring; showy
M	17. Consolidated	Q. Without stopping
O	18. Pandemonium	R. The killing of a king
L	19. Vigorously	S. Tightening
T	20. Reluctant	T. Unwilling

VOCABULARY JUGGLE LETTER REVIEW GAME CLUES - *Bridge to Terabithia*

SCRAMBLED	WORD	CLUE
TRIG	GRIT	backbone; determination
ANSEBGH	SHEBANG	the whole thing
TELELICAYD	DELICATELY	sissified manner
YDGUP	PUDGY	chubby
DDLMUED	MUDDLED	confused
GEYCA	CAGEY	tricky; sly
TIOCSOLANON	CONSOLATION	comfort
LTERFAED	FALTERED	hesitated; wavered
OMSLYINOU	OMINOUSLY	threateningly; darkly
SONLEM	SOLEMN	serious
YEGALRL	REGALLY	stately; dignified
RGEEVEN	REVENGE	to get back at; punishment
IGSLYOROUV	VIGOROUSLY	energetically
IDGICERE	REGICIDE	the killing of a king
CRONIMS	CRIMSON	deep red
RPLUSUS	SURPLUS	extra amount
UNFNGODLI	FOUNDLING	abandoned infant
DATEPERES	DESPERATE	hopeless
PSCBEDRERI	PRESCRIBED	assigned; designated
NEDINLIC	INCLINED	known to; tendency
UCRTANTEL	RELUCTANT	unwilling
EGSDR	DREGS	remains
GHARSI	GARISH	glaring; showy
VECALO	ALCOVE	recessed opening
LEVI	VILE	mean; disgusting
GEDOBLI	OBLIGED	grateful
STUYANCAR	SANCTUARY	place of worship
TACSPELEC	SPECTACLE	public display
NGCOPIRNSI	CONSPIRING	plotting

www.ingramcontent.com/pod-product-compliance
Lightning Source LLC
Chambersburg PA
CBHW051411070526
44584CB00023B/3377